Forewc

Pipe Major Evan Macrae BEM was tau͟
the Isle of Skye, and joined The Queen's Own Cameron Highlanders as
a boy piper in 1938. During World War II he went to India with the 1st
Battalion of the Cameron Highlanders in 1942, and was appointed Pipe
Major in 1944 during the Burma campaign. After the war he graduated
at the famous Pipe Major's Course at the Army School of Piping and
gained a 'Distinguished' grading.

He then held the appointment of Pipe Major of the 1st Battalion of the
Cameron Highlanders for an unprecedented 13 years, serving in Great
Britain, the Far East and Middle East, Austria and Germany. His
leadership earned universal acclaim for the high standard of piping and
turnout for which the Cameron Highlanders Pipes and Drums were
celebrated. After leaving the Regular Army in 1962 he continued his
Regimental service as Pipe Major of the Liverpool Scottish TA until
1967.

In 1974 he retired to Lochaber where he became Piping Instructor to the
Education Department of the Highland Region, and was a key figure in
the remarkable resurgence of piping in the Camerons' home territory.
He was awarded the British Empire Medal for services to piping in 1987,

and his legacy continues to this day in the Lochaber Schools Pipe band. He closed his competitive career on the highest possible note by winning the Gold Medal for Piobaireachd at Oban in 1982.

Evan Macrae's memoirs are a unique personal account of a life devoted to piping in the Cameron Highlanders, and to encouraging the young pipers of Lochaber.

Donald Cameron of Lochiel, XXVII Chief of Clan Cameron

September 2020

INTRODUCTION

By

Duncan Macrae

This is not a war book, nor does it contain details of any war action; there are many other books that do justice to this genre. No, this is a memoir of a man who grew up with bagpipes, became a piper, served through several military conflicts while being a piper, and ended up giving back as a gift to others, his love of the highland bagpipe. That was his raison d'etre. To be a piper. I first became aware of Dad's memoirs when he was ill with cancer, but had not seen them. When he died my mother gave them to me in the hope I would make some attempt to have them published, as was my dad's desire. There have been a couple of attempts to put them into a formal document but now that I am retired, and we have been locked down as a result of the Covid-19 pandemic, I have had a great opportunity to complete it.

As I said, this is not a war story but a collection of experiences he had from growing up in Skye and the West Highlands to finally retiring in Fort William, where he ended up as a peripatetic tutor of bagpipes. I apologise for any errors but am only putting down what Evan wrote in his handwritten notes. When compiling this I realised there are many stories he told me which have not been included – this may be because they are writer's licence, or inaccurate in detail, or purely made up for a young boy's ears. Like for example his story of how and why the soldiers dug latrine pits in the jungle, or his first experience in a New York strip club, or the night he and another piper visited a cinema. They are some of the memories I have of his experiences. At his funeral, at which there seemed to be hundreds I realised then he was a different man to so many people. He was a father, husband, granddad but also a soldier, musician, and teacher.

ACKNOWLEDGMENTS

I would like to thank the following people for their assistance and advice in getting this book completed.

Tom Peterkin, from the Press & Journal; Jeannie Campbell the Piping Historian who also writes for the Piping Times; Stuart Letford, Editor of the Piping Times; Dr Decker Forrest of Sabhal Mor Ostaig; Cameron MacFadyen the Skye Piping Convenor and also Piping Tutor in Skye; Ian Grieve from the Scottish Highland Games Association; Edward Usborne the Secretary of The Queens Own Highlanders Association; Duncan MacDonald an ex Cameron who took over as Piping Tutor in Lochaber after Evan; Terry Nigh from W.J.Nigh & Sons Ltd who own copyright of the postcard produced by J. Arthur Dixon; Lt Colonel Angus Fairrie (retired) ex Cameron who provided some text from Evan's obituary and of course Cameron of Lochiel for his foreword.

Contents

Chapter 1 - Braes, Brose and Bothies 1922 - 1929

My birth certificate states that I was born in the Upper Corrie, in the parish of Urray, Ross-shire on 21st February 1922. The Corrie is on a hillside overlooking Muir of Ord which is on the Black Isle. In later life when asked where I was born I would answer Urray and would notice a blank look on the questioner's face. I'd then quickly say Ross-shire, and their face would show amazement and they would exclaim 'Russia!'. It must have been the way I said Ross-shire.

Sometimes I'd say I was born in the Black Isle, which in fact is not an island, and that would take an even longer explanation.

As I had lived most of my young life on the Isle of Skye, I would claim Skye when asked where I came from.

My parents had moved to Stranraer after I joined the army. During and after the war, if my picture appeared in the paper, normally at some piping function, I'd get remarks like,

'I see you come from Stranraer, I thought you were born in Skye!'

In the end, I let them think what they pleased as I got fed up explaining the long story.

The other slight irritation was the spelling of my name, especially south of the border where I was McCrea, McCree, MacRay, etc, everything but Macrae. In fact my brother Oliver eventually spelled his name MacRae - this seemed to suit his style of writing. I wonder how many other Scottish names were changed through mis-spelling. And I would apologise to any people mentioned here whose names I misspell!

My father was a forester, or woodman as they were called in those days, and I first saw daylight in one of the wooden bothies which were erected for the woodmen and their families wherever their next felling job happened to be.

I remember visiting there in 1977 with my brother Oliver. He was the eldest in our family of four, and we were accompanied by my wife Molly and Oliver's son Gordon.

Oliver knew exactly where to go and when we approached a farmhouse on the hillside he said,

'A Mrs. Tuach used to live here.'

We knocked on the door and it was opened by a sprightly old lady in her nineties - the same Mrs. Tuach.

We explained who we were and the purpose of our visit. She was delighted and I can still hear her voice in that soft Ross-shire accent,

'I remember the day you were born' she said to me, 'Your mother and I were great friends, and your father Duncan was such a big strong man.'

She suggested we take a walk up the hill and see where the bothie had been, then come back for something to eat. My brother Oliver was fourteen when I was born and he was able to point out the exact spot. Also where the dam had been which supplied water for the steam engine that drove the sawmill.

My father had been the saw miller and Oliver the fireman - quite a heavy job for a boy of fourteen. The stumps of the trees that had been cut 55 years earlier were still there and nothing had been done with the land since.

Woodmen worked hard in those days and did not have such machines as tractors and power saws.

They were also hard-drinking men, and of course, my father like the rest was fond of a dram. He used to talk about those days in later years when he and I would be having a quiet drink during one of my leaves from the army.

I remember one New Year celebration when we lived in Skye, when my father had that wee bit too much, getting told off by my mother. He was storming out of the house shouting that he was going to drown himself and the reply from my mother was,

'Well take off your good shoes, they'll fit one of the boys when they get older!'

Such was my mother's sense of humour, which I appreciated more in later years.

My mother was a small woman but strong in body and mind which stemmed from a hardy Caithness upbringing. Right up to the age of eighty, when she died, she would tell me some funny story about years gone by.

From the Corrie, my father moved to Rosehaugh on the Black Isle as a sawmiller on Fletcher's estate. That was where I first went to school although I was only four. My sister Hilda, two years older, was of school age and I was told that I screamed the house down to be allowed to go with her. I don't remember much about it, but the school was in Killen, a couple of miles inland.

My father had joined the Scots Guards in 1904 but was on the reserve when the 1914-1918 war broke out. He was sent out to France and Belgium, where he was wounded and captured at the Battle of Mons. I am sure it had not been a very pleasant experience for him and others like him, being a POW for four years, and he

carried an undying hatred for anything German for the rest of his life.
A German family once called at our house in Skye looking for a
room for their summer holiday and his words were,

'There's no bloody German coming into my house!'.

They never got past the garden gate!

Like my mother, he too had a sense of humour, but was also a strict
disciplinarian. I suppose their sense of humour brushed off on me, as
I have great fun listening to other people's humorous stories. We
would sit around the fire and listen to his stories, and one, in
particular, was about the time he worked with other prisoners on a
farm in Germany. They were using the old fashioned flails to thresh
the grain. Three of them and the farmer's wife were beating to the
frau's counting - 'ein, zwei, drei, vier...' then she would tell them to
stop so that she could turn the sheaf over. One day she forgot to say
stop and bent down. My father being number 'ein' brought his flail
down on her head...so it was back to the camp for two months
punishment and no farming.

I enjoyed his army stories and there was another one he told of the
time he was stationed in Chelsea Barracks, London. The
Metropolitan Police used to drill regularly on the barrack square.
They were drilling one afternoon when a Scots Guardsman stuck his
head out of the window and shouted,

'Fat bobbies on the left, thin bobbies on the right, short bobbies in the
centre, in two ranks size!'

The outcome was the Guardsman being doubled into the guardroom with the punishment of fourteen days confined to barracks. It was never revealed who that guardsman was!

I think my father got tired of the woodman/sawmiller business for we did not stay long at Killen. But long enough for me to hear and remember my first sound of the bagpipes at the funeral of James Douglas Fletcher in 1927. I still wonder to this day who the four pipers were that played the lament, for they stirred something in my young mind that remained with me until I was able to know what it was all about.

As my story unfolds, the reader will realise how much bagpipes have affected my life.

This same year saw my father on the move again. This time to estate work on Castle Leod at Strathpeffer. I remember the short stay there was very pleasant and we lived in a cottage at the back of the old meal mill at Millmain. The mill worked every day then and to a young boy like me, this was something wonderful, watching the whole works driven by the big water wheel. We always had a plentiful supply of oatmeal so it was brose or porridge every morning. I recall my father trying to make some sort of beverage out of bruised oats, something I suppose he had learned in the POW camp. I don't know if it had been a success. By now, I don't think my father was drinking as much, as he became very successful at gardening, and there was more opportunity for him, now that we were out of the bothies.

The farm next door was owned by a David MacIntosh, a kindly gentleman who let us wander around his fields and farm providing we did not disturb his crops. The dam that drove the mill was at the back of our house and it was there that I learned to fish. Hilda my sister, Sandy my brother (two years younger) and I always roamed around that dam, and we knew exactly where all the coots and water hens made their nests. Sometimes there would be great excitement when we would get a visit from a couple of swans. There was no such thing as vandalism in those days and the birds around the dam were never disturbed.

The big hill Knockfarrel was half a mile from our house and we would walk across the fields to get to the base. When the weather was fine we would climb Knockfarrel and we could get a wonderful view of the valley from Strathpeffer to Dingwall and the serpentlike River Peffry. There is no railway there now, but in those days there was a line between the two towns. Strathpeffer did not have a turntable and the engine used to reverse all the way back to Dingwall. My father used to joke with us suggesting we go to the railway line and make faces at the driver,

'He'll throw coal at you, which will help with the fire.'

Chapter 2 - Over the Sea to Skye 1929 - 1936

To my mind, we seemed to be happy at Millmain and I never knew the reason why my father left Castle Leod Estate, but the next move was to the Isle of Skye, where my father was to take over the job as a handyman on Lord MacDonald's Estate in Armadale, which is in the south of Skye.

To a boy of seven, Armadale estate had everything one could wish for - a big castle, plenty of trees, a field with plenty of rabbits, and only half a mile up through the trees to the place we knew as Sunset Hill, where we could see plenty of deer. When I later discussed our move to Skye with my sister, who is two years older than me, she remembered the journey from Ross-shire to the Isle of Skye. My mother had a Rhode Island Red hen (which she named 'Granny') and a brood of chickens in a basket, which she carried with her to the island. This was my mother's thriftiness being put to use; whatever happened, when we got to our new home, she was going to have her hens and be sure of a supply of eggs. I mention her thriftiness and her Caithness upbringing, only because, I suppose this helped to bring us through the tough times that folk had to endure in those days. She had two brothers who emigrated to Canada after the Great War and became successful farmers. Through talking to my cousin Rose, who was born in Canada, I learnt of the hard work that they experienced before becoming successful. Rose's father, William, played the bagpipes so it must have been from my mother's side that my interest came, as there were no known pipers in my father's family.

17

We were not rich, and no hope of ever being so, living in Skye, but we were happy and my father worked hard to ensure we did not go hungry. As the months went by my mother's hens began to lay, and we would be sent to the local shop with a couple of dozen eggs to help pay for the weeks' groceries. I also became proficient at setting rabbit snares in the field in front of the house. I would have to go out at dusk to set the snares and then check them in the early hours of the morning - this was to avoid being caught by the Gamekeeper, George MacKay, a nice gentleman. Thinking back now, I don't suppose he would have said anything had he caught me at my little act of poaching, which was to help the week's rations. There was no myxomatosis then, and my mother had her special way of cooking rabbits. It was a meal I can still remember to this day.

It has been said that the Skye people take a long time to accept outsiders, but not in our family's case. We were accepted immediately, and offers of help came from all parts of Armadale and Ardvasar. I loved the Skye folk and still do to this day and I still enjoy a visit there to see the people who I knew as a young boy. The Sabhal Mor Ostaig, which is now a Gaelic College and a working farm in my young days, organise a piping school each Easter, so I've been able to visit the place, as an instructor at the school, since 1976.

Numerous people befriended my family, among them, Davy MacLean and his wife Lena, Neil Kennedy who had the Grocer's shop, Jimmy (Beag) McInnes, his wife Ina, Angus the 'post' (Jimmy Beag's brother), and Colin Nicholson and his sister Alice. Their father Lachie worked with my father on the estate and our mothers were friends.

One other person who I must mention is the Ardvasar Blacksmith, John MacDonald - He was my hero!

I used to watch him shoe horses and to see John shape a lump of iron into whatever form he wanted was magic to me. He also made Cromags, or Shepherd's Crooks, out of hazel or ram's horn.

He was also the local piper and no ceilidh in the village hall was complete without a tune on the pipes from John.

I went to school in Ardvasar, which was about a mile from where we lived. No such thing as school buses in those days, and in the good weather we would run to school barefoot, after a good bowl of brose and a 'switched' egg for breakfast. For our lunch at school we would have a jam piece - certainly nothing fancy but we never went hungry.

There was always the danger of bad weather in the winter with Macbrayne's boats not being able to call, so we had to be well-stocked with an ample supply of flour and meal, for scones and oatcakes. And a barrel of salt herring kept in the shed at the back of the house.

Sunday was always the day for the special dinner, but we had no visiting butcher's vans, so my mother had a regular order of beef sent from Riggs the butcher in Inverness. The beef would be boiled and a big pan of broth made with our home-grown vegetables, which would last two or three days. As I said, we were poor but we did not starve and the food we had was wholesome. Sweets and toffees were treats that appeared at Christmas.

I enjoyed my school days in Skye and had the same teacher for eight years; Miss Harriet MacMillan from Benbecula. There were never more than thirteen pupils at that school in Ardvasar all the time I attended. I always believed Miss MacMillan to be a good teacher. She found time to teach us Gaelic and Gaelic songs as well as our normal subjects. Among the subjects taught were geometry and algebra, and the boys were taught gardening.

Miss MacMillan was eventually awarded the MBE which to me was a well-deserved award.

With working in the woods and sawmills my father became an expert saw-doctor. The crofters would come for miles to get their saws sharpened. There hadn't been anybody in that area for years who could sharpen saws and he would have a laugh at the state of some of them. I've seen him file out a new set of teeth on them, such was the state of wear.

It would be my job on a Saturday to deliver the saws and a six-mile hike around the crofts meant nothing to me. When I delivered the goods, it wasn't just 'thanks' and 'cheerio' - I would be invited in for something to eat which was normally a big plate of potatoes boiled in their skins, salt herrings, followed by homemade scones or oatcakes washed down with a pint of milk fresh from the cow that day. Knives and forks were never used, potatoes and herrings were picked with the fingers!.

Although I understood the Gaelic language, I never really learned to hold a conversation. The Skye people knew this, and although Gaelic was their everyday tongue, they were such nice folk that they always spoke in English when there was a non-Gaelic speaking person in their company.

Ah! Such was life on Skye as a schoolboy.

One school holiday I got a job in Armadale Castle as a kitchen boy - skinning rabbits, plucking hens, looking after the boiler house - but it was just a seasonal job, as the Castle was closed during the winter months, except for two elderly lady caretakers. The people who rented the Castle brought their own staff with them and if I remember correctly they all came from England and Wales.

In 1935 my Uncle William from Paisley came to visit us in Skye and took me back to stay with them for a month which was very exciting for a boy who had never seen a big town. We drove from Kyle through Lochaber and across Rannoch Moor, camping out a couple of nights, which was great fun. But, a month was enough and I longed to get back to the island, even though I enjoyed the luxury of the ice-cream van stopping outside my uncle's door every day.

Uncle William had a flute in the house which I took an interest in. One day he said to me,

'If you can play a tune on that thing before you return to Skye, you can have it, for good!'

I worked at it, and before returning to the island I could play The Glendarual Highlanders. He stuck to his word and I still have that flute to this day!

I had now reached the age of fourteen and time to leave school. There wasn't much work for youngsters of my age on the island, so most of them went to the mainland to seek employment. There was always a relative or some contact in one of the big cities to assist in these cases. My sister, Hilda, had left two years earlier to live with an adopted aunt in Edinburgh until she could start her training as a nurse.

However, I didn't have to go just then, as Bert McKenzie, (now a well-loved councillor in Staffin), had Armadale Farm and told my father that there was a job for me on the farm if I wanted it. That job was to feed the cows, muck out the byre, harness Tommy the horse, and cart the manure to the fields. I had great fun with that horse! He knew exactly where to stop when I was dumping the manure in the field and would move on again without any prompting.

Bertie was good to me, and his wife Mrs. McKenzie used to put some excellent meals on the table, and seconds if required.

I also had a terrible yearning to be a sailor, so I had played around with boats as often as I could. If there was somebody local with a rowing boat going out to their creels or to fish in Ardvasar Bay I would always ask to go with them. From that, I picked up the art of sail.

During one summer holiday, I got a job on the local ferry, which was owned by two brothers. It plied between Armadale and Mallaig three or four times a day and I earned half a crown a week(12.5p). One evening, I think they must have had a wee bit too much to drink, a fearful argument developed on the last trip home to the island. I had to row the dinghy ashore that evening after the ferry had anchored. When I told my father about it, I was sorry, as he put an end to my mariner's days.

Chapter 3 - A Musical Introduction 1936 - 1937

The army had a drill hall in Portree with a regular army Sergeant Major, who recruited the length of the island. He visited Ardvasar one evening, I suppose looking for recruits for the Queens Own Cameron Highlanders Territorials, the Regiment of Inverness-shire, which Skye was part of. My father was lured to the village, excited by the visit of a soldier from the regular army. (He still spoke of his days in the army. In fact, there was an old 78 rpm record of the Trooping of the Colour on Horse Guards Parade and any visitors to the house would have to sit in silence, as he took us through the whole procedure. He had his own words to the Slow and Quick Marches)

He returned to the house that evening with the Sgt Major - Tommy Cameron - for a cup of tea and the usual homemade scones. He told us that he had got two new recruits, Jimmy Souter (who has since passed away) and Angus Nicholson, who still lives on the Isle of Skye and were both three years older than I.

Tommy Cameron said to me,

'How would you like to join?' but my mother in my defence said,

'Och! He's too young, he's only fourteen'.

The Sgt Major suggested that I could enlist as a boy piper. At last, things were happening, the idea of becoming a piper got me very excited, and if he had asked me to go that night I would have had no hesitation! My father was quite happy to let me join and between us, we eventually persuaded my mother that it would not do me any harm.

In due course, we, Jimmy, Angus, and I were driven to the Drill Hall in Broadford which was about fourteen miles from Armadale, where we were sworn in.

Every week there appeared a car to take us there to drill. This came easy to me, as Hilda, Sandy, and I were taught foot and arms drill by my father, from as far back as I can remember, using wooden rifles he made for us at the sawmill. We loved this as youngsters and I suppose my father got a kick out of it as well.

Our mail delivery was in the evening and there was great excitement when a parcel arrived for me with a label, "On His Majesty's Service" addressed to 2929356 Boy E. Macrae. It was a practice chanter and the music for the Regimental duty tunes, sent from Pipe Major William Young who was stationed in Inverness at Headquarters. Perhaps I should explain that a practice chanter is the instrument that one must learn before going on to the bagpipes.

The next move was a visit to the blacksmith!

John MacDonald seemed pleased to take me on and insisted that I learn the music from the start.

I enjoyed my visits to John; some nights he would give me a lesson in the smithy, sometimes in the house, and I was never sent home without a drink of milk and some scones. The first tune John taught

25

me was *'Over the water to Charlie'*. Little did I realise then that I was going to hear it played every day for twenty-five years!. It was the tune that the duty piper played when dinner was ready, but the troops called it *'Keep a big dinner for Geordie'*.

I worked hard at my finger exercises and looked forward to my next lesson from John. He was known as Iain A'Ghobha by the local people, which is Gaelic for John the Blacksmith. His way of life had never changed. He is now (at the time of writing) over 80 and still keeps a couple of cows for fresh milk, still works his croft, and can still pick up the pipes and play a good tune. He never misses going to Church and in my young days, he would be seen walking or cycling the two miles to Kilmore Church every Sunday. He used to lead the singing for the Gaelic service. John has never had a television but has a radio and is well up in the world news. I visit him every year when I go to the Sabhal Mor and he never ceases to surprise me with his vast amount of knowledge. I never know what he is going to surprise me with next. I went to see him one Easter and he produced a miniature set of bagpipes, made from locally grown laburnum and turned on a foot lathe. A true Highlander who has never changed his lifestyle from a strict upbringing, this was the man who started me off on my piping career!

If I may give a word of advice, at this point, to any up and coming young pipers, no matter where you go to seek advice to further your knowledge in piping, do not forget the person who started you off and gave their time to set you on the right track. I know John looks forward to my visits every Easter, although he is very modest about how much he taught me and always says,

26

'It must hae been there in the first place!'

Chapter 4 - The Boy Piper Enlists 1937 - 1938

Time was drawing near for the Territorials to go to their annual two weeks camp at Nairn. I arrived home one day from the farm to find my mother in tears and my father using language I had never heard him use before. My mother explained that he had had a row with the estate boss. I was worried about seeing my mother so distressed, so I mentioned the incident to Bertie MacKenzie the next morning. After lunch, Bertie gave me a paper to take home to my father. I don't remember now what paper it was, but it had advertisements for various jobs. Bertie had pencilled off one of the jobs - it was for a gardener/handyman at Aratornish Estate in Morvern, Argyll. My father sent off his application and he was eventually invited to go for an interview at Oban. He was successful at the interview and was offered the job, but I know he was very sad at the thought of leaving Skye.

There were three weeks from the time my parents left Skye and my going to Camp at Delnies, Nairn, so Bertie said I could stay with him until I 'went off to the Army', as he phrased it.

It was also very sad at my leaving the island for good, as we all had hopes that one day we could have our own croft, and my parents spend their last days on Skye.

There was great excitement the morning I left, getting dressed in kilt and spats, a big breakfast from Mrs. MacKenzie, and a parcel of sandwiches that would have kept Tommy the horse going for a day!

28

A bus trip of twenty-two miles to Kyleakin, the short trip on the ferry across to Kyle, then the train journey to Nairn and my first taste of army life.

The camp was under canvas and each man had a mattress filled with straw and three hairy blankets - no such things as sheets. The 4th Battalion The Queens Own Cameron Highlanders were a good Regiment and trained hard while they were at camp.

Although I was an enlisted boy I still practised with the older pipers. This was my first meeting with Pipe Major Young, the man who had sent me the chanter and music. I was a bit apprehensive of him, he looked so tall and fierce in his uniform and waxed moustache. I need not have worried, as he was a gentleman. Although he had a band of twenty-four pipers to look after, he still found time to sit down with me as a learner and give me lessons. The bandsmen came from all over Inverness-shire. They were a good band and the Pipe Major had a way of putting them 'into shape' as he used to say when I got to know him better in later years. He had a lot of influence on me when I reached the stage where I was qualified to teach piping myself.

I remember there were some fine men and good pipers in that band - the three Macrae brothers from Blackpark, Inverness; Dan, Sandy, and Archie. Dan went on to be Pipe Major of the 2nd Battalion Camerons, fought at the Battle of Cassino, and will be remembered for his beautiful composition *The Heights of Cassino.*

Another piper in that band, Dan MacDonald, took over as Pipe Major of the 4th Battalion in France and was captured at St Valery in 1940. After the war, he taught the Army Cadet Pipers.

Two other pipers with whom I became very friendly were from South Uist - Angus MacKay and Donald MacIntyre. The former was an uncle of the famous piping family from Glenuig, Dr. Angus, Allan, and Iain MacDonald. Angus MacKay was one of the first in the Battalion to get killed at St Valery in June 1940. Donald MacIntyre was captured at the fall of France and spent four years in a prisoner of war camp. After the war, he became Pipe Major of the Territorial Battalion which was then renamed the 4th/5th.

Another member of that band, William MacDonald of Kingussie, after the war made a big study of Piobaireachd (the classical music for the bagpipe) and succeeded in winning both the Oban and Inverness Gold Medals.

I enjoyed life at that camp and I loved to hear the band playing reveille. The weather was beautiful with not a drop of rain. We were well fed and as a boy, I was entitled to a pint of milk a day.

The Battalion was preparing for a fourteen-mile march to Inverness, with an overnight stay at the Cameron Barracks. The Pipe Major said I was too young for the march so I was left behind to look after his dog "Flirt". The Pipe Major's job was a gamekeeper at Dochfour Estate and I think Flirt was his favourite working spaniel.

I left camp two days before the Battalion, as I now had to travel to Lochaline in Morvern, to where my father had moved. The journey to Oban was via Stirling and Crianlarich, a beautiful trip I remember, but sadly that line is now closed. I arrived in Oban too late for the ferry to Lochaline, so I had to look for a place to sleep for the night. I think I paid three shillings (15 pence) for B&B at the Bayrien Hotel and got the first ferry in the morning. It seemed an awfully long journey to me at the time, but in later life, I was to travel for three days across India. No comparison really but I suppose to a boy of fifteen it would seem long.

Lochaline was a beautiful place but somehow I felt more cut off from the mainland than I did when we lived on Skye, although geographically Morvern is the mainland.

The only employment that I could get in this area was with the Forestry Commission. As a boy, I started at sixpence (2.5p) per hour which later rose to seven pence (about 3p) per hour. The first task I was given was quite pleasant and the weather was good. We had to row across the loch to a forest, measure the girths of the trees, chip off a piece of the bark, and stamp the trees with F.C.S. (Forestry Commission Scotland). I worked on this for a week with the local Commission boss, Mr. Drysdale, who was later to give me a reference when I decided to join the regular army. This was an easy job, but as the summer drew to an end, I was sent out to the hills above Lochaline, to drain the high ground and prepare it for planting. It was heavy going and all drains were dug by hand with a big cutting spade, then hauling the turf and heather out with a three-pronged rake type of tool and then turning them over so that they made a soft bed for the young trees to be planted in.

There were men on the Forestry Commission who had come from St Kilda. I'll never forget one day during my short stay with the Commission. I was working with one of these men, he was on the cutting spade and I was hauling out the turf. Some remark he made prompted me to say the wrong thing in answering, being young, and possibly a bit cheeky. He lifted the draining spade and would have hurt me had I not moved quickly. I dropped the tool I was using, ran, and hid in a wood nearby until I saw them going home at five o'clock. I never told my parents and when I returned to work the next day nothing was said of the incident. However, it was a warning to me to be careful about what I said in the future! The man concerned was very friendly to me from that day on.

As the year 1937 drew to a close we started planting where we had drained. The young plants were carried in a bag slung over the shoulder. A small spade was used to make a 'T' shape in the soil and opened up for the tree to be planted, then heeled in. This was interesting for me until the weather changed and the sleet and snow started to blow across the hills. We all arrived for work one day and could not leave the hut, there was such a blizzard blowing. We kept ourselves warm with flasks of tea and sandwiches. At three o'clock in the afternoon, we were told to make our way home. There was no way that we could cycle through that blizzard, so we had to push our bicycles the four miles to Lochaline through two feet of snow. When I arrived home my hands and feet were aching. Just about in tears with the pain as I was beginning to thaw out, my mother said,

'I don't think you should go back to that job'.

But the idea of losing the few shillings I was earning did not appeal to me.

However, the next morning, as if my mother had second sight, the mail arrived and there was a letter addressed to 2929356 Boy E. Macrae with the usual O.H.M.S on it. It was from Sgt. Major

32

Tommy Cameron who had left Skye and had rejoined the 1st Battalion Cameron Highlanders in Catterick Camp, Yorkshire. He stated in his letter that there was a vacancy for a boy piper in the regiment. How good I felt, thinking that there was only one vacancy for a boy piper and that I should be the one to fill it!

Incidentally, I found out later that those letters were sent to boys all over Scotland and some selected schools.

In a way this was the answer to my mother's wishes, not to go back on the cold hills. I was going to be a full-time soldier, not just for two weeks in the year.

The recruiting posters I had seen at camp came back to mind, of soldiers in their smart uniforms, pipers in full regalia, I was going to be one of them!

I did not go to work that day as there was a lot more snow on the hills and when my father came home in the evening my mother told him about the letter. He pondered over it for a while, then asked me what I would like to do. I could see the look of happiness on his face when I said that I would like to go. He warned me that I would have to sign on for nine years and that he could never afford to buy me out if I did not like the life. It was a case of making your bed and lie in it. My mother suggested that I might wait and join the Scots Guards, '...like your father', but he said,

'No, you'd never stick the discipline.'

He was a loyal guardsman and always thought there was no other regiment like them. Little did he know that the Camerons were as

33

strictly disciplined a regiment as the Scots Guards, which I was soon to find out when I got to Catterick - the Pipe Major, Iain MacLean, a native of Mull, had come to the Camerons from the Scots Guards! You only had to make one false move on parade to realise how much a disciplinarian he really was.

The letter was duly answered, stating that I wished to enlist.

Christmas 1937 and then New Year went by and no reply from the regiment. Then a letter came later in January inviting me to go to Oban recruiting office to be sworn in.

Back home to Lochaline and wait for the next correspondence.

It finally arrived with a rail warrant. I was to go to Stirling Castle, the depot of the Argyll and Sutherland Highlanders. My father was a bit worried about this and he warned me,

'They will try and shanghai you into the Argylls, so if they don't let you go to the Camerons, tell them that you left a good home and that you can always go back to it.'

I was kept in Stirling Castle for five days in a cold room high up in the building. I can still remember the wind and the coldness in that room in January 1938.

There was another boy about the same age as myself and he was enlisting in the Argylls. John MacKenzie was his name and I didn't see him again until we met at Verden, Germany eight years later, when we were rehearsing for the Victory Parade in 1946. He was Pipe Major of the 2nd Battalion Argyll and Sutherland Highlanders and I was Pipe Major of the 5th Battalion Camerons. John eventually became Pipe Major in Queen Victoria's School, Dunblane.

Only once was I asked if I wanted to change my mind and join the Argylls and I gave them my father's answer!

Chapter 5 – First Camp 1938

On the fifth day, I left Stirling Castle for Catterick Camp and was met at Richmond Station by Corporal Peter MacIntosh from Nairn, who eventually finished his career as a Sergeant Major. I was taken to the cook-house and a substantial meal put before me by Paddy Cairns, the cook Corporal who was as large as he was jovial. We became great friends in later years.

Then I was taken to the boys' barrack-room to meet the Drum Major 'Jock' MacPherson, Corporal Peter Scotland and Corporal George Allan who were in charge of the boys. The first boy to welcome me was John MacLellan, who eventually retired from the Army as Captain in charge at the Army School of Piping, with an MBE.

Life in Boy Service was very strict, bed at half-past nine every night, except Wednesday, Saturday and Sunday when we were allowed to go to the Garrison Cinema.

Reveille was at half-past six in the morning, with a hot mug of tea, then in shorts and vests, (cardigans in the winter) socks and boots, there would be a road walk and run for half an hour. Back to the barracks and into the showers – it was hard going but one soon got used to it.

Schooling was most important for Army Boys and we attended every day, learning map reading, regimental history, and a book to read for the English exam. The book we all got to read was Greenmantle by John Buchan.

There were three exams one could take as a boy – 3rd Class, 2nd and 1st but not many had the time to take their 1st Class before leaving Boy Service. There were a few, mostly who had come from Queen Victoria's School, Dunblane and had started their army training at the age of ten. One of those boys who I was friendly with for years was Alex Sandilands, a good piper and highland dancer. Highland dancing was another must for every boy and we had some fine instructors in the Pipe Band.

There was also plenty of sport, football, hockey and boxing. I liked playing football but I never played much in my earlier school days. Shinty was my game but never played in the Army. I always remember my first game of hockey. Every move I made was a foul, lifting the hockey stick above the shoulder. I never got it right until later days in India and Tripoli.

All the boys had to learn to box but the Pipe Major put a stop to it as he said it was bad for the hands. We used to have instruction from a young blonde Lieutenant Maitland-Makgill-Crichton, who was referred to as babyface by the boys, but never when he could hear it. I'll never forget watching him box in the ring, for he was an expert with the gloves and his opponents never lasted the three rounds with him, he had such a knockout punch! He was one of the great soldiers that the Cameron Highlanders produced and retired from the army with the rank of Major General.

The part of the training I really enjoyed was the piping instruction and although I'd been seven months away from camp at Nairn I'd practiced a lot. I knew all the duty tunes when I got to Catterick.

I dreaded meeting the Pipe Major as I'd been warned how strict he was. He came from Mull which was just across the water from Lochaline. He interviewed me; I think he accepted me and asked about my family. Also, the fact that my father had been in the Scots Guards pleased him and I believe he had a soft spot for me. I remember him saying to me when I went home on my first leave

'Don't you be telling the people back home in Lochaline that I'm bad to you, as I'm well known there'

He also had a soft spot for John MacLellan – maybe he saw into the future for us. He would let us borrow his own books, particularly Pipe Major Ross's Collection which contained tunes he wanted us to learn for competition. He was a good man but as I said a strict disciplinarian. He was killed early on in the war but had he lived, no doubt he would have been proud of the young piper boys that he had taken such an interest in.

April 1938 was the date for the battalion to go to Bellerby, out on the Yorkshire moors, for the troops to spend a month there doing their range practice on all weapons and to receive their proficiency pay. It was here that the Pipe Major gave me my first set of bagpipes. I was delighted and after morning drill it was practice for the boys. I remember getting away from the camp where I couldn't be heard. It didn't take me long to master them and when I returned to Le Cateau Barracks, Catterick Camp I was put on the duty piper's roll.

The duty piper's role was to play reveille, breakfast pipes, dinner, tea and Officers Mess. Dress for dinner at half-past seven and then at eight o'clock when the meal was ready we would play Bannocks of Barley Meal.

The last call of the day was lights out. Sometimes there would be guard mounting where the piper paraded with the guard on the Regimental drill parade ground. We would be inspected and march the new guard to the guard-room, then play the old guard off.

I remember making a mistake on one occasion on guard mounting and the Regimental Sergeant Major shouting

'Stand still that piper, you're stupid enough to be a Pipe Major'.

I met him in a pub in Inverness after the war, he'd been promoted to Major. I reminded him of the remark he had passed when I was a boy. However, I informed him that I'd made it and was now Pipe Major. We had a good laugh and a few pints that night.

Summer came and a month in Leeds for the Military Tattoo. I wasn't competent enough to play with the massed bands but was a torchbearer during the performance. During the day I was a waiter in the Sergeants Mess. We were under canvas in Roundhay Park and I think it rained every day during the Tattoo, so the white spats had to be scrubbed after every show, dried by braziers and re-blancoed for the next evening. There was no dodging as every man and boy was inspected before the evening parade and performance.

We returned to Catterick Camp and I had learned most of the band tunes, so I was allowed to play in the band for the first time. How proud I felt, happy being able to practice with the band and marching at the head of the Battalion every Sunday to Church. There were some great men in that band, to name a few Johnnie Auld, accordion player and piper, Snook Allan, who went through the Burma Campaign and retired from the Army as Regimental Quarter Master Sergeant. Also Norman Scott the Pipe Sergeant and highland dancer who later became Pipe Major. One name I must mention here was Donald MacDairmid. Donald had served in the Argylls for a long time before joining the Camerons. He fought in the South African War and First World War. It broke his heart when he was told that he was too old to go to France in 1939. He was sent to the depot in Inverness where he died never having had a civilian suit in his military life. His last duty was looking after the Sergeants Mess and I do not doubt that they looked after him well also. I can still see him marching through the barracks straight as a ramrod, the Regimental Crest worn off his buttons with so much polishing, Glengarry perched at the correct angle and the waxed moustache. Donald would spend every evening in the canteen and the pipers would always make sure he wasn't short of a beer.

John MacLellan and I were also sent to Inverness when the war started as we were too young to go to France. I remember hearing Donald playing me the tune Sprig of Ivy on the chanter. A beautiful tune, but very seldom heard these days. He had a good memory and a great repertoire of tunes. I also remember the night I bought him a bottle of beer in the canteen and he said

'You'll be a Pipe Major one day'

He never lived to see that and died in Raigmore Hospital, Inverness. Quite a character!

1938 was the crisis of the Munich Agreement which was designed to avoid war between the powers of Europe by allowing Nazi Germany under Adolf Hitler to annex the Sudetenland in Czechoslovakia. Every boy and man were set to digging air-raid shelters, but the crisis died down as suddenly as it had started.

During my stay at Catterick, I got my first leave home to Lochaline. Wearing the complete Piper's uniform, belts, dirk and eagles feather I was also allowed to take my pipes with me.

My father met me as I got off the ferry boat and I know he was pleased with what he saw – the shoes, buttons and belts were all inspected.

There would be a tune on the pipes every night after the evening meal, then sit around the fire. He would ask me all sorts of questions about army life, some I could answer, but there were a few I couldn't. He was delighted with the progress I'd made on the bagpipes and although he never played them, he loved to listen to them. One of his friends in the Scots Guards was Alec Ross, brother of the famous Pipe Major William Ross.

It was soon time to return to Catterick and I can still hear his lecture as we waited for MacBrayne's Ferry Boat to Oban. He explained an old local man had died of cancer. This was the first time I'd heard the word and my mother had told us it was an incurable disease. He warned me to be careful and keep away from women who chased after the soldiers, or I'd get a disease worse than the old man had died of.

After a few weeks back in Catterick I received a letter from my mother informing me that they were on the move again and Dad had got a new job further away from the highlands on Logan Estate, Wigtonshire as sawmiller/gardener.

Chapter 6 – A Visit Home to Family 1938 - 1939

Just about this time the Battalion was ordered to move from Catterick to Malplaquet Barracks, Aldershot.

So December 1938 saw us all going on Christmas leave. I vaguely remember having to spend the night in the Union Jack Club in London and getting the early morning train from Euston to Stranraer, a long and monotonous journey

I arrived at Stranraer but there wasn't a bus for Port Logan until ten o'clock that night. My mother had told me to tell the conductress to let me off at Logan Estate gates but omitted to tell me that there was a two-mile walk through the estate forest to our house. The long walk through the estate woods carrying a suitcase, bagpipes and dressed in full Highland garb was not a very pleasant way to start a Christmas leave. And I was still only sixteen years old...

However, I followed the road and got to the big house, Logan House and rang the front doorbell. It was answered by the cook and I suppose being half asleep and not very amused, her directions got me to the gamekeeper's house.

He was quite pleasant for he knew my parents had been expecting me. Again a wrong turning and arrived at some farm cottages, awakening one of the farmhands. By this time I was only two hundred yards from my parent's house

43

I knocked at the door, the paraffin lamp burning with its familiar smell and everybody got up to welcome the soldier home. When I say everybody I mean Mother, Father and younger brother Sandy. My sister Hilda was away training to be a nurse at the Southern General Hospital in Glasgow and Oliver had left home in 1933 to make his living in England. He'd got a job as 'Boots' (a worker employed to clean boots, shoes and carry luggage etc) in Kenilworth Castle, going on from there to Footman and Butler, the job he was doing when war broke out. He had also joined the RAFVR (Royal Air Force Volunteer Reserve) and was called up in 1939 at the very start. I think he only got home twice on holiday before the war but I was able to meet him when the band had an engagement at Leamington Spa.

Oliver was like my young brother Sandy and took his height from our mother. My sister and I were a bit taller like our father. My father's brother Evan, who I was named after, was six feet seven inches tall and died at the age of seventeen – they say he had grown too fast and had a weak heart. Oliver and I had two entirely different lifestyles. He was a deeply religious man, taken from our mother and although I was a God-fearing person I didn't work at religion, like him. We were brought up to attend Sunday school and church regularly when we lived in Skye.

There was one thing we had in common, a great sense of humour. When I would go to visit him in Glasgow where he settled after the war, he would accompany me to the pub and while I would be drinking whisky and half pints of beer, Oliver would sit with a glass of lemonade and listen to my stories. Hard drink never touched his lips.

He was always ready with a witty answer and I recall one instance when Sandy's second son Angus was born, Hilda said 'the baby had a right head of black hair', to which Oliver asked 'what colour is the left one'

He then worked at Singers, Clydebank and on his retirement moved to Fort William as he had a great love for the highlands. Also, his daughter Morag lived there. We had great plans for the future as he was a keen photographer and had hopes of doing the round of Highland Games with me. He had been to the Portree Highland Games with me before his retirement and he enjoyed it immensely. We'd spent the night with Murdo MacDonald of Borve, Skye, another great soldier who went through the Burma Campaign, was wounded but survived.

Alas, our plans for the future never materialised as Oliver died in his sleep on 4th April 1978. He always said that he was on borrowed time as he had had a heart operation in 1960 but he still hiked the hills around Glenfinnan and also part of Ben Nevis.

After he died arrangements were made for him to be buried in Kilmallie Churchyard. However the day before the funeral, Gordon, his son, discovered a note in Oliver's Bible of his wishes, if he had died in Drumchapel. He wanted to be cremated with his ashes scattered in the Glenfinnan area and for me to play the tunes My Home and The Rowan Tree. There was also a request for his favourite hymns to be sung at the service. The arrangement for burial had already been made so it was impossible to have the remains cremated, as his wishes were discovered too late. I did play the tunes he requested at the graveside. He now rests on the hillside in

Kilmallie Churchyard overlooking Loch Linnhe, Ft William and Ben Nevis, the places he loved so much.

I felt the usual sadness which is normal in any family bereavement, but when the minister Rev Edward Lewis from Drumchapel St Andrews Church spoke of Oliver's great contribution to the church I felt a certain proudness which eased the sadness. He would have been delighted to know that his two grandchildren were learning to play the bagpipes. His son Gordon although had been to University and studied Chemistry, following his father's death would go on to study for the Ministry. This would also have been a delight to his father.

Chapter 7 –Back at Aldershot 1939

I enjoyed life in North Camp, Aldershot and we used to go for walks at the weekend on Farnborough Common where we saw the famous Spitfire for the first time.

There was always plenty of sport and inter-regimental football matches. There was no dodging, everybody had to parade and with roll call taken, we were marched to the football field. However there used to be some good matches and although we were forced to go, everybody enjoyed watching their team, especially when they would win. Glengarries would be thrown in the air but you always had to watch where it would fall or you could finish up with a hat that was either too large or too small.

It was in Aldershot that I entered for my first piping competition.

The piping judge that day was Pipe Major Andrew MacIntosh, late of the Scots Guards and who owned a pub The Rose & Crown in Chelsea. I did not know then but found out later that Andrew had worked with my father in a sawmill at Kiltarlity, Beauly.

The prizes were presented that day by Mrs Wimberly the Commanding Officer's wife and she asked me where I had learned my piping. When I told her it was on the Isle of Skye she wanted to know which part. I answered Armadale in Sleat and she asked if I knew the Kembles of Knock. I'd never met them but one of the family had served in the Scots Guards with my father.

47

The next competition was open to the Aldershot Garrison and I got second in my group. The boy who got first prize was Alec Couples of the Gordon Highlanders. He finished his career as Pipe Major of his regiment.

Buckingham Gate, London was the next competition and the event I played in was the Boys March. The tune I played was The Taking of Beaumont Hamel. My bass drone had slipped down and Pipe Major MacDonald of the Highland Light Infantry, tried to signal to me to tune my drone up, but the nerves got the better of me and I was in too much of a hurry to get my tune over and done with. No prizes that day!

Pipe Major MacDonald was the father of William MacDonald Benbecula, (well known in piping circles and a gold medallist) who served with me during the last two years of my service in the Cameron Highlanders.

This was the first time I had met K. G. Roe of the Scots Guards or Curly as he was affectionately called. He was on the prize list that day and a very fine player. He too attained the rank of Pipe Major in his regiment. Curly departed from this world in 1976 aged only 55 years old.

I used to enjoy the church parades along Queens Drive to St Andrews Garrison Church, but one Sunday when returning to barracks the band had stopped for a breather when my chanter fell out onto the road. Pipe Major MacLean turned around and shouted

'Corporal Colquhoun, put that man in the guardroom when we get back to barracks'.

My whole life and happiness collapsed at that moment and the dread of spending all Sunday in the cells really frightened me.

However, when we were dismissed from parade the corporal called for an escort to march me to the guardroom, the Pipe Major had changed his mind, and it was just a severe ticking off about the care and maintenance of the bagpipes. Throughout the rest of my service, this mishap never happened to me again and I used to warn young pipers about making sure that their chanters were secure in their instruments.

In 1939 a new order was issued that boys would join man service at the age of seventeen and a half instead of eighteen, so I left boy service on the twenty-first of August 1939. In boy service, we weren't allowed civilian clothes, but I had saved up some money and with a few pounds sent from my mother I bought my first civilian outfit. I didn't have them for long though as the war broke out thirteen days later on 1st September 1939 and all civilian clothes had to be sent home. I moved into the men's barrack-room and was now Piper Macrae.

A five-day route march was organised for the young soldiers of the battalion, mostly recruits just arrived from the depot in Inverness and a small band of eight pipers, all under nineteen.

We set off on 1st September, marching all day along miles of Hampshire lanes and sleeping in bivouacs made from two groundsheets and a couple of poles. The same followed on 2nd September. After breakfast on Sunday morning, we marched for about an hour and when we rounded a corner there was a convoy of troop-carrying vehicles waiting to take us back to camp. War had been declared.

As could be expected there was great excitement when we returned to barracks. Who was going to France? Who was too young or too old to go across the Channel with the British Expeditionary Force? It wasn't long before it was sorted out and those not eligible for France were sent to a place called California, which looked like a summer holiday camp. I believe this was California Country Park in Berkshire. This was so that the reservists being called up could be accommodated. Some of these poor reservists had only been out of the army for a few weeks, some of them having served in India and the Middle East for years and here they were back in uniform.

The Home or Rear Details, as we were called returned to Malplaquet Barracks after the battalion went away to France. We were all put to work digging air raid shelters around the barracks and married quarters.

After a couple of weeks digging, I got a job as Brigade Messenger. This entailed going around various regiments with official mail on a heavy army push bike. I was certainly fit and had muscles on my legs like a racehorse peddling that bicycle.

It was at this time that the 4th Camerons passed through Aldershot and were stationed next to us in Tournai Barracks. I visited them and met up with my old friends from my camp days in Nairn. But there was no Pipe Major Willie Young. He was too old to go to France and was put in charge of the pipers at the Depot in Inverness. The man who replaced him was Pipe Major John Wilson who went to Canada after the war and did so much for piping over there.

Orders were issued in November that all Rear Details were being posted to Inverness where we eventually arrived and billeted in the original Northern Meeting Rooms.

Chapter 8 – Training in Inverness 1939 - 1942

There were a lot of young soldiers in the Meeting Rooms and we were formed into a demonstration platoon. We had all sorts of weapons training and drill under RSM Jock Slee on the Cameron Barracks square. John MacLellan and I were in this platoon but not for too long as Pipe Major Young had heard that there were two young pipers in 'F' Company in the Northern Meeting Rooms, just arrived from Aldershot.

He requested that we are sent to the barracks and this was the second time I felt apprehension about this great man. When we reported to him he asked me my name and where I came from. I told him and his response was

'you're the bugger that stole my chanter!' 'No Sir', I replied, 'I haven't stolen it' and produced it. He left it with me but unfortunately, it got broken two years later.

Soldiering in Inverness as a piper was good but hard as we would be out on route marches with the recruits in all weather. We got marvellous piping tuition from Willie Young and every second day there would be a new tune on the board. He was always ready to teach piobaireachd (pibroch) to any piper interested.

There was a wonderful bunch of pipers in that band and I must name them here as every one was a character in his own right.

Donald Stewart from Lochmaddy who taught me little tricks on the care of and how to wear one's uniform. He was always immaculately dressed.

Hugh (Shug) Fraser from Kingussie, an outstanding player who eventually became Pipe Major of the Royal Scots after the war.

Jimmy Hughes from Maryhill, Glasgow, a good piper, soldier and comedian. I can still laugh when I think of "Jimmy's patter" and his Glasgow humour. Jimmy did twenty-two years with the Camerons; his last job before retiring from the regiment was Recruiting Sergeant. You just have to mention Jimmy Hughes to any piper who served in the Camerons and some funny incident would be recalled. I remember when we were stationed in Spittal, Austria 1953 there wasn't a married quarter large enough to house Jimmy and his family of nine, so they had to live in a family Hostel. We were playing at an Officer's Mess guest night and Jimmy, he was Corporal Hughes at that time, was one of the three pipers playing with me. The main guest that night was General Urquhart of Arnhem fame. When the dining room was being cleared the General came out to talk to the pipers, as most guest officers did at those functions. He mentioned to Jimmy about his big family and having to live in the Hostel. Jimmy's reply in his Glasgow accent was

'Aye sir, every time I tak' ma troosers aff the wife's expecting'

The General had a sense of humour and had a good laugh at the expression. Jimmy was my Pipe Sergeant in Korea 1955/57. There used to be dull evenings in the Sergeants Mess but not with Jimmy about. He kept us all going with his patter. I could write a whole book about Jimmy Hughes.

Then there was Donald Matheson who survived the Burma Campaign and eventually settled in Canada.

Ginger Moran and that strong Barra man Willie MacNeil who had spent some time lumber-jacking in Canada. Ginger and Willie had the habit of going out on the Walleroo (cheap wine) on a Friday night, headhunting as they called it. They were regularly arrested by the Military Police and spend the rest of their weekend in the guardroom. I needed to visit Barra in 1976 and went to see Willie, we had a good catch-up, unfortunately, he died on New Year's Eve 1981.

Willie MacCrostie was also in the band, called up with his age group. He was another great player and always willing to give help and advice to young pipers. He was a kindly man and he eventually became a reed maker. When I started making reeds in later years Willie was only too delighted to help me with anything I wanted to know.

Angus MacDonald from North Uist, another good player, left the Depot to become General Wimberley's personal piper in the new 51st Division (the original 51st Division were all captured at St Valery and spent the war in a prisoner of war camp). Angus then took over the 5th Battalion Cameron Band and when he left he joined the Glasgow Police as Pipe Major. He retired from the force as an Inspector.

Robert MacKay or Micky as he was known was another outstanding piper and also a good footballer. Micky managed to get back from France and joined us in Inverness. He took on the band of the 7th Battalion Camerons, which later became the 5th (Scottish) Parachute Battalion. He won both Gold medals, Oban and Inverness after the war.

Willie (Blindo) Wright, good piper and excellent dancer who also had a wonderful sense of humour. Willie Young used to cycle into Inverness from Scaniport and home again, a total distance of about twelve miles. I remember Blindo asking Willie Young if he could borrow his bike, Willie's reply was

'You can borrow my wife first'

It was during this time that Malcolm MacPherson son of the famous Angus MacPherson, Inverness came to the regiment and we used to hear some beautiful music from Malcolm's instrument. Both light music and Ceol Mor.(literally 'great music' to distinguish piobaireachd from more popular lighter pipe music)

The firing range for the recruits was at Daviot south of Inverness and each squad was accompanied by one piper when they marched to the ranges, which was six miles from the barracks. The piper would play from halt to halt, fifty minutes marching and ten minutes rest every hour. We would stay overnight at Daviot and march back to the barracks the next evening. We all had a large repertoire of tunes but I remember the Pipe Major saying that if we ran out of march tunes to try playing reels in march time. I tried it and it worked.

Then there would be the all-day route marches around the Culloden area, Loch Ness over Abriachan or round by Bunchrew and Kiltarlity.

The only man who never complained of sore feet was Willie Young. After marching all day he would get changed into his tartan trews and cycle home to Scaniport.

During that time James Mackintosh joined the regiment as a boy soldier and was obviously going to be a piper of the future, which he proved in later years, winning both Inverness and Oban Gold medals.

Tam Pentland was also a boy soldier at this time and joined the regiment from Queen Victoria's School. He was my last Drum Major in the Queen's Own Cameron Highlanders and was an outstanding drummer. He also learned to play the bagpipes which is a great asset to any band – a Drum Major who could play the pipes. We were great friends and it was a sad day for me when he passed away at the age of forty-seven on 22nd April 1974. His wife Margaret had been a Warrant Officer in the WRAC. She was certainly a daughter of the Regiment – her father was Percy Dodds, who I met in 1960. He could tell a good story and had been a drummer in the Camerons when they served on the Rhine after 1st World War

A Lieutenant David Murray walked into the barrack-room one evening and asked for a blow on the pipes. The pipers thinking here is somebody who thinks he can play as had happened so often in the pipers' barrack room. The pipers sat back and listened. When the officer struck up, they were all amazed by what they'd heard, for they were listening to a man who had been taught by the famous Robert

Reid and William Ross. Typical of a piper's way of thinking, one piper remarked

'What is he doing wasting his time as an officer, with fingers like that?'

This same officer went on to serve 20 years with the regiment and retired with the rank of Lieutenant Colonel. He was later for a time deputy producer of the Edinburgh Military Tattoo and from the 1960s until the 1990s he was a frequent voice on BBC Scotland's various piping programs.

There were no pipe majors' courses during the war but there was a specific month's course for pipers and pipe majors alike to go to Edinburgh to receive tuition from Pipe Major William Ross. I was fortunate to get on one of these courses and I became very friendly with Robert Reid's brother Tommy who was Pipe Major with the Royal Scots Fusiliers.

Returning to Inverness I was posted to Nairn as 'C' Company piper. At first, my duties were route marches, Officers Mess dinner nights and the company dances to play for the reels.

The cottages behind the Marine Hotel down by the sea, where the pipers tune their pipes at every Nairn Games, was the Officers Mess. I used to like those nights and the favourite dram with the officers was Glenfiddich. I never got too bad and was always able to find my way home in the blackout to the Annexe behind the Highland Hotel where I was billeted.

It was at one of the company dances when I was playing for the reels that I met the girl, Molly, who was later to become my wife.

I was friendly with a reservist called Paddy Rooney who had served in India in the twenties and had been a keen sportsman, one of the regimental sprinters, also a drummer. When he was dancing with Molly he asked her if she knew of a Sandy Tweedie from Nairn, who was his pal when he served in India. Molly told him that Sandy Tweedie was her uncle. He was delighted and after the dance, I was called over and introduced to Molly and her sister Jean. The next dance was a ladies' choice and Molly came for me. I wasn't much of a ballroom dancer, but she insisted she would teach me. From then on romance blossomed and I was eventually invited home to the house. Molly's parents were good to me and there was always a meal when I visited them and a packet of cigarettes slipped in my pocket. Molly's sister used to play the piano so there was always a sing-song in the house and there were many Camerons invited to the house. Soldiering in Nairn was pleasant.

When I think of the route marches from Nairn one incident comes back to me. I was company piper and we were about four miles out of Nairn on a narrow country road when we came to a Y junction. It was the officer's job to point with his Cromag (like a swagger stick) which way he wanted me to turn, as I was playing at the head of the march. The young officer failed to do this, so I turned left, but the company turned right. I marched for about ten minutes when I sensed nobody was marching behind me. I had to run back to catch up with them. It never happened to me again, as I would always stop playing when we approached crossroads.

I was then given a different job; as well as being company piper I was to be Sergeants Mess barman and Mess waiter. I also had to move my billet to Moray Place which was in the centre of High Street, Nairn.

I didn't like the Sergeant's Mess work very much and the cook and I slept in one morning, which meant the Sergeants going on parade without breakfast. We were both charged. The cook received seven days confined to barracks and I was sent back to Inverness. I was happy to get back to the band as there was so much I could learn from Willie Young, but I was sorry about leaving Nairn and my girlfriend. However I could get a Saturday night pass and there was always a shakedown (floor to sleep on) in the front room for me at 3 Water Lane, Nairn.

Shortly after I returned to Inverness it was decided that the barracks were to become a Training Depot for the A.T.S. All troops were moved to Fort George eight miles away, but the Pipe Band, Military Band, drivers and some administrative staff were to remain but billeted in the Millburn Distillery, which was just outside the barracks. It was a cold billet, and we ate and slept there, but still did our practice in the barracks. We still carried on with our duties as pipers, doing drill parades for the girls. Route marches were regular and not as long as we did with the troops, but at a quicker pace.

We were allowed to use the same N.A.A.F.I. canteen as the girls, so we used to have some fun in the evenings. Jimmy Hughes could always be expected to keep the party going.

The B.E.F.(British Expeditionary Force) was having a rough time on the continent and the whole thing collapsed after Dunkirk, which is well written about.

The 1st Battalion, or what was left of it were stationed in England. They were being strengthened again, so Donald Stewart, 'Shug' Fraser and Donald Matheson were recalled to the battalion.

John MacLellan left to become Pipe Major of the 9th Seaforth Highlanders.

It was at this time that we had a fright. Willie Young was cycling home to Scaniport when he was accidentally shot with a .22 rifle. The bullet had gone through his chest but did not damage any organs. He was hospitalised for a long time so Willie MacCrostie, who was a Corporal then, took over the duties as Pipe Major. He'd earned his Pipe Major's certificate before the war. He carried out his duties very well and we played at some nice guest nights in the Officer's Mess. We also broadcasted for the BBC under Willie MacCrostie's direction, playing some of Willie Young's compositions.

During my stay at Inverness I had about three leaves home to Stranraer and by this time my father and brother Sandy had joined the Home Guard. Sandy was a Signaller and my father a Drill Instructor. When I came home after the war I was amazed at Sandy's knowledge of Morse Code. I was in a pub in Port Logan during a leave at the time my father died in 1951 when one of the locals told me that he had argued with my father about some drill movement. He told me that my father had said to him

'I was drilling when your backside was the size of a shirt button'.

Sandy had wanted to enlist and get involved in the war but he was a farmworker so was exempt. This was a sore point with Sandy, for I knew how much he wanted to join and do his bit, but he wasn't nineteen until 1943.

Willie Young survived his accident and was soon back in charge of the band. At the beginning of March 1942, he walked into the band practice room and said

'Well, Macrae they want you back in the 1st Battalion'.

I knew "they" as he called the powers that be did not ask for Macrae especially, but it was his way of breaking the news that I was about to join the war effort. I was then 20 years old. It didn't worry me unduly as I knew I would be alongside some of my old friends and it had always been in my mind that I wouldn't be able to stay in the depot during the whole of the war. Arrangements were made for my leave and travel, with the usual farewells. The old Colour Sergeant Tommy Mitchell who looked after our pay and Jock Slee the RSM also bid me farewell and good luck.

So it was with full kit, big pack, kit bag and carrying a Ross rifle I was sent home on two weeks leave before joining the battalion at Adderbury Barracks near Banbury. Jimmy Hughes came to the station to see me off. He was a bit downhearted as we had been such great friends. He said he hoped to follow me. He eventually did get out to India but was posted to the Seaforth Highlanders and went into action with them in Northern Burma.

Leaving home after that 2-week leave brought tears to my mother's eyes but my father was hard, he had done it all twenty years before.

He wished me luck and said I'll see you on your next leave. That was to be four years later.

Chapter 9 – Life at sea 1942

Walking into the pipe band hut in Adderbury was not strange to me. All the pipers who had left Inverness before me were there and some of the pipers who had managed to get away at Dunkirk – Sammy Hall, Davey Allan, Deeks Downie and of course Norman Scott who replaced Pipe Major Iain MacLean in France. Dan (Snook) Allen had also survived Dunkirk but was not with the pipers at that time. He was in the Motor Transport later being transferred to the Mortar Platoon.

There were a couple of new pipers I'd never met before – Jimmy Williamson and Cushie Cousins. Jimmy was great friends with Sammy Hall and he eventually settled in Canada. I met up with Jimmy in 1978 when I went with Molly for a holiday to Canada. Jimmy and his wife Jean spent the weekend with us.

There was a move on and everybody was getting excited about it. I remember thinking here were some of the men who had gone over to France, taken a pounding and were now looking forward to getting into action again.

Security was good and nobody had any idea where we were headed for.

I had a short stay at Adderbury and it seemed a very quiet place. However, I did have time to visit some of the local pubs with Donald Stewart, Shug Fraser and Donald Matheson.

Orders were given for the regiment to pack up our kit and stand by. Rumours were rife and there were all sorts of guesses and assumptions. Tropical kit and sun helmets were issued so it was somewhere in the East.

At midnight on the 11th April we were called on parade, the roll called and marched across some fields to the railway station. It was a moonlit night with frost and snow on the ground.

Travelling all night we had no idea where we were headed for but there were some fine fellows from Liverpool who recognised the countryside and knew that we were going to Liverpool. These lads had come from the Liverpool Scottish which was affiliated to the Cameron Highlanders.

We sat on the Liverpool docks by the troopship MS Marnix Van St Aldegonde a pre-war Dutch Liner.

The advance party had boarded earlier and were throwing bars of chocolate to us. I don't know where they had acquired it but it was grey and musty. However, the men on board ship were eating it so we were not too worried about it.

We eventually got on board and issued with a hammock and blanket. This was slung over the mess decks from which we ate during the day.

It was very uncomfortable in these hammocks as we were crammed into such a small space but all the troopships were the same and after all, it wasn't a pleasure cruise we were going on.

Reveille was at six o'clock in the morning and all hammocks had to be stowed away on a special rack provided so that they looked neat and tidy when the ship's Captain and our Commanding Officer accompanied with their followers did their daily inspection.

We'd set sail from Liverpool on 18th April. It was a dull foggy day. As we sailed out of the harbour we could see some of the docks still smouldering from a previous air attack. When we got to the mouth of the Mersey River we saw the huge convoy of ships and their escorts. The convoy began to get into formation. It was fascinating to watch the escorts nipping about the convoy at terrific speeds and I loved to watch them. We sailed down through the Irish Sea and zigzagged well out into the Atlantic but by now we knew by the sun and change of temperature that we were heading south.

The first port of call on the West African coast was Freetown, Sierra Leone but we did not get ashore. The ship refuelled here and we were off again south.

The pipers and drummers were formed into an anti-aircraft platoon, so were assigned to man twin Bren guns in two pits aft of the ship. We had now passed the Equator so we could sleep on deck at nights now. The pipers used to spread their hammocks under the gun pits and life seemed a bit more pleasant at this time. We never saw an angry plane or any U-Boats so we didn't have a chance to fire our twin Brens but they were still checked and maintained every day. The only gunfire we heard was the naval gun mounted at the stern of the ship having target practice.

There was a lot of fun and banter on the journey. Somebody had said that the Sergeants Mess was having a snooker competition. Some poor gullible soldier would be sent to the sharp end of the ship to find a stone, as a cue ball.

I remember on that journey a story told by Jimmy Williamson, which I still laugh at. One drummer who was known as "Tell the Tale" had a bugle that was a bit bashed and had been telling some of the Royal Engineers who were travelling with us that his bugle had been in the South African war. He wasn't one of our best buglers and when he went to blow his duty call, one Engineer was heard to say

'Listen to that awful sound! It was definitely in the South African war!'

The convoy now reached Capetown and we were taken to Retreat Camp a few miles outside of Capetown. We did not have any weapons and very little equipment, as it was only for three days.

There was a march from the camp which included a climb up a steep hill. Boots had to be worn to keep our feet in shape, as we had been wearing nothing but plimsolls on board the ship. I suppose this was to protect the decks and boot studs could be dangerous on metal stairways.

There was no special formation to get to the top of that hill; the order was just to get there somehow. There were trips into Capetown and the band entertained in the centre of the town one evening.

Shug Fraser had relatives there so he, Donald Stewart and I were invited to the house one night. There was a young lady there who took a shine to me and asked me to write to her when I reached my destination. I also had the address of an elderly WVS lady who had driven us up to Table Mountain, who also wanted me to drop her a line.

When we did finally get to India I wrote to both ladies but got the addresses mixed up, and as expected no answer. Maybe I made an elderly WVS lady very happy that day.

We moved off around the Cape to Durban where there was a shortstop to put off a seriously ill soldier, then we were told the news. Our destination was to be Bombay, India.

Chapter 10 – India 1942 - 1944

On arrival at Bombay, there was the usual wait around for our kit to be offloaded then on to a troop train bound for Poonah. On the 12th June, we arrived at Kirkee railway station at about midnight and during the monsoon season. We were formed up with two pipers at the head of each company and a guide with a lamp in front to lead the way. We arrived in Pashan Camp in the early hours of the morning and had to erect our own tents. There were laughs, groans, swearing, and some screams that night. As the tents were being unrolled some poor soldier was stung by a scorpion, which crawled into it, probably to escape the rain. We were told that a raw onion rubbed on the wound was a good cure. But where could one get a raw onion at that time of night?

Soup and tea were soon on the go and we eventually got our tents erected somehow.

Next morning looking at the camp it was as if it had been hit by a hurricane. However, the day was confined to fixing the tents, lining them up properly and digging ditches around them to keep the water away.

This was the first time that I'd seen Char Wallahs, Fruit Wallahs and various other tradesmen who had passes to visit the camp. The Dhobi Wallahs would take your laundry away in the morning and bring it back in the evening starched and pressed. I could never understand how they could tell the difference between each man's laundry, with just a little mark they put on with India ink.

The monsoons eased up and the camp was looking good, but it was time to move on. I can't remember who took over that camp from us but they certainly got a better bargain than the Camerons got when we moved in.

From Pashan Camp, Poonah we moved to Ahmednagar northeast of Poonah where normal training carried on as usual. Pipers were always in demand for route marches. The billets there were straw huts but we got used to them.

It was a short stay there and our next move was to Allenby Barracks in Secunderabad. These were pre-war stone-built barracks with electric fans and punkahs (Indian ceiling fan) to keep us cool. There was a swimming pool in the barracks so we spent as much time as we could in it. There was a good canteen where there were all sorts on the menu. Also beer, but it tasted like vinegar.

We had our normal orderly piping duties and officer's mess nights. One night Shug, Donald and I were playing with Pipe Major Scott, when an argument broke out. Shug and Donald were both put in the guardroom. I was shocked as I never thought anyone would talk back to the Pipe Major. Shug lost his Lance Corporal stripe and Donald got seven days confined to barracks. All the band members felt sorry for them but they did not complain. They were old soldiers who had already served in India before the war and took their punishment without a moan.

By this time each company began to claim their own piper so I always went to 'C' company. The Company Commander was Major Roy and the Sergeant Major, Tommy Cook. It was in that company that I met Murdo MacDonald from Borve in Skye and we became great friends. There was a great competitive spirit between companies and we had a marching, shooting and drill competition during our stay in Secunderabad, which 'C' company won.

I was on a route march with them one day when we marched by another company resting by the roadside. Tommy Cook shouted to his opposite number

70

'have you got some water?' and was questioned 'Are you thirsty Tommy?' 'No' he replied, 'I want to blanco my equipment at the next halt'.

This was the spirit that kept the battalion going through the two years of hard training in India, and then on to the battles in Burma. Tommy Cook kept himself fit and was a good boxer. He was not a drinking man but every New Year's Day Tommy would send for his "company piper" as he called me and he would have a big dram for me. Tommy was killed in action before the battle of Kohima in the thick of the fighting. He had been awarded the DCM but was killed before he could be told. In 1960 Tommy's widow died in Edinburgh and her relatives asked if I would play the pipes at her funeral. That evening Tommy's medals were presented to the Sergeants Mess.

Training got harder as the months went on, Brigade exercises, Divisional exercises, Combined Operations with the Navy and intensive jungle training. The first jungle training we did was at a semi-hill station Mahabaleshwar. It rained all the time we were there and as we had taken pipes and drums with us there was no place to keep the instruments dry. An American Missionary was living in a bungalow near the camp and he gave permission for the instruments to be stored on his veranda. I got the job of looking after them. The Reverend Long was his name and I used to get coffee, hot pancakes and honey every morning while I stayed at that bungalow. I was able to keep dry during the month while my mates were soaking wet all the time and I took a lot of leg-pulling after that.

There would be sing-songs around the fires at night and it was the first time I'd heard Captain Peter Grant sing Gaelic songs. One song, in particular, I remember hearing him sing was Caberfeidh.

Then came our first aquatic exercise on a lake at high altitude in Kharakvasla north of Mahabaleshwar. The boats we trained with were a type of lifeboat with every man on board manning a lever to work the propeller. This was small fry compared with what was to come.

We moved to a camp on the beach at JuHu near Bombay. At first, we all had to swim in shorts only, then gradually added more items of clothing until eventually, we were carrying everything in the water. If there was no training on a Saturday we would get a day pass into Bombay. I used to like going to the bazaar, normally with Donald Stewart. He could haggle with the merchants and usually got the better of the bargain. We would spend the rest of the day at a swimming pool and in the evening frequent the canteen run by WVS where we could get tickets to purchase a couple of bottles of beer. Donald always found a way to get extra tickets so we normally finished up with more than just two bottles. The last train back to camp was a laugh for there were a few of the Jocks who had the same idea as Donald for getting extra beer. Sore heads on a Sunday morning were easily cured for it was just a few yards down to the sea, and a half-hour swim.

There was also an Assault Course at that camp which really took some getting through. It was never known for anybody to fall out on that course as our previous training had kept us all fit. I do remember one piper Sam MacPherson from Inverness carried a scar throughout the war from a rope burn he had got on that.

It was on one exercise during this when I was on the same boat as David Murray who was in charge. He told me that when the boat touched bottom I was to jump off and play the charge. I duly obeyed the order and when I jumped off, the water reached my armpits. As company piper, I had to wear kilt. This was a new experience for me seeing the kilt floating all around me as I waded ashore!

I played the troops ashore but spent a miserable day marching as the kilt dried on me with my thighs and legs red raw with the rubbing of the wet kilt.

Tam Hyde, another company piper had the same experience as me on his boat and he was shorter than me. There was nobody like Tam in producing a brew of tea on an exercise and all the other company pipers would seek Tam out during a break as they would be certain to get a drink of tea. Tam had survived Dunkirk having joined before the war but I didn't get to know him until 1942. He was a keen piper and you could always hear him practising when everybody else was resting or in the canteen.

He had the trick of appearing on parade with his brew can and stove concealed from the inspecting eye. Long after I left the army I went to visit Tam at his place of work. I was taken into the visitor's room and given the best of treatment. He worked for Drambuie in Edinburgh!

Our first long exercise from JuHu was with the Royal Navy along with all the troop and vehicle carrying boats. Again I got lucky. I was ordered to go to the Admiral's ship as General Philip Christison was on board and naturally being an ex-Cameron Highlander he wanted a Cameron piper.

He was a fine man and I used to give the Gaelic toast after I played on the Officer's mess deck. He once asked me where I had learned my Gaelic and I said Skye. My Gaelic wasn't that good and the only Gaelic he heard me speak was the toast, which had been taught to me by Donald Stewart.

It was on the Admiral's ship that a Royal Navy man asked if he could have a blow of my pipes. He struck up and started to tune them. His tuning phrases were familiar and he was a good player. I asked him where he had learned to play like that and he said the 2nd Battalion Cameron Highlanders.

Training at JuHu was over and the next move was to a place northeast of Bombay about 22 miles – Bhiwandi. An all-day march along the pipeline to a camp in a valley where I've never known heat like it. Our pipes were drying up so we had to put damp towels round them to keep the reeds moist. Even at night, we had to put the pipes on a groundsheet and cover them with wet towels.

During this training period Gandhi's people were causing trouble and at an hour's notice company or battalion could be on the move. On one such move, the band went with Brigade HQ to a camp outside Ahmedabad, where the locals had not seen British soldiers for years. The few words of Urdu we knew were not understood in this part of

India. We spent four weeks at that camp and one night we were having a campfire concert when I heard a Military Policeman whistling a Gaelic air. I found out that he came from Harris and was a cousin of the butler on Logan Estate where my father worked. His other cousin lived at Bunchrew and was an officer with the Cadets after the war.

The Pipe Major had acquired a hunting rifle so we used to go out hunting blue bull (Nilgai) and also pigs around the villages. There were no objections from the locals as the blue bulls were destroying their crops. I've never known to this day if they were wild pigs or if he had paid the villagers in advance to be allowed to shoot them.

On our second visit to Ahmednagar, I was given the job as Officer's Batman to Lieutenant Quarter Master Alec Leckie and Captain Bobby Arnott. I didn't like the job but it was an order and I carried it out to the best of my ability. I had two good friends who were also batmen. John Irvine, a pre-war piper and Sticky Kennedy a clever tenor drummer, who used to fascinate everybody who saw him put on his masterly performance with the sticks. Sticky had been abroad before the war and had the Royal Family tattooed on his back. When he returned to India this time he had his tattoos brought up to date.

One day the Pipe Major approached me and said 'I want you to apply for promotion to Lance Corporal' but I did not think much of being an NCO (Non-Commissioned Officer). I also didn't like the idea of filling Shug Fraser's shoes who was a good friend and a better player than me. The Pipe Major gave me twenty-four hours to think it over. The next day he approached me and warned me that if I did not take this promotion I would be a batman for the rest of my life as a

75

soldier. The application was made out, recommended by the Pipe Major and I received my first stripe. The entire band knew what was happening and when I walked into our hut wearing my stripe, nobody would talk to me. It was just a prepared gag and it only lasted until the evening. I couldn't even celebrate my promotion with my depot pals as I now had to use the Corporals Mess. There were the normal duties of a young NCO which I picked up easily and I gained confidence as the weeks went by. Roll call, parade, inspections, marching out to do marker for the band. But it was strange – if there was anything I was worried about I never asked another NCO, but would always talk to Donald Stewart. He always seemed to have an answer to my problem.

Christmas and New Year arrived and Donald and I were detailed to play in the Sergeant's Mess. We prepared a good programme and the Sergeants seemed to enjoy it. There was plenty to drink and as we found out to our cost, too much!

Just as we were preparing to leave the Mess having had our share of the Christmas spirit, a vehicle pulled up outside the Mess with two young officers in it. They had also been celebrating.

'Come on Macrae and Stewart, come along with us to the Officer's Club and wake these Sassenachs up!'

This seemed a good bit of fun so we were told to strike up when the doors opened and march in playing Pibroch o' Donal Dubh. We started alright but when we tried to march the drink that we had consumed earlier was now taking effect. We did not march, we staggered around the floor.

The Provost Marshall was present and when he saw this spectacle he ordered the Military Police to remove us. It took five of them to persuade us to get into the back of the truck, with Donald shouting

'Come on Eóbhan', he never called me the English version Evan, 'get stuck into these Sassenach bastards'

We found out later there was actually only one Englishman amongst the five Military Police. We were thrown into a cell with only one bed. When we woke in the morning, New Year's Day, we could see onto the veranda through the cell-door bars. There was a Harris man on sentry duty, an old soldier named MacCauley and every time he passed by our cell door he would whistle the Cameron Men. Word had got around that we were in the guardroom, so Shug thought he would visit us, complete with a bottle of whisky and wearing a pith helmet. He was having a good laugh at us, so Donald called him over to the bars. Donald pulled the sun helmet off his head and through the bars and proceeded to jump on it. That helmet would never see another parade.

After many conferences, the outcome to this episode was that the two young officers took the blame for the whole affair, so we were released that day after a ticking off from our Company Commander Major Preston. I was forever grateful to those two young officers for their kind act as I could have been demoted and Donald confined to barracks for a very long time. It wasn't so much being confined to barracks, but the chores that one had to do while undergoing punishment was no easy task under the burning sun. Sadly one of these officers was killed at the battle of Kohima.

Gulunchi and Visapur were two other stations where the battalion underwent intensive training and there was more time for sport like inter-company boxing, football and athletics. Organised cross-country running was the big thing in Gulunchi and it was a must for everyone. The regiment was divided into three packs – fast, medium and slow, with the Commanding Officer in the fast pack. There were no villages or bazaars near these stations but everybody seemed to be in good spirits.

It was at Gulunchi that a light aircraft had to make a forced landing in our camp. It came down on our football field but overshot and went through three tents killing several of the occupants. A military funeral was arranged in Poona. The band was turned out complete with muffled drums, playing The Flowers of the Forest. It was the first military funeral I had experienced with the band and it seemed very sad, but something about that music and the drums remains with me to this day. After the service, the battalion marched away from the cemetery at the slope arms with the band playing a lively march.

During our training at all these stations, the band would find time for chanter and band practice. Later when I was promoted to Pipe Major I would think of the difficult job Norman Scott had with the pipers and drummers having different jobs throughout the battalion. He was always cheerful and he never let it get him down.

He was an expert on weapons and loved handling them. The battalion formed a general reconnaissance platoon and they were taken away from the battalion for a while to train in the wild, living off the land and learning new tactics. I think Norman was teaching them the art of sniping. I remember going to his cabin on the troopship out to India and he was testing a silencer which he had made for a .22 rifle.

My two friends Donald Stewart and Murdo MacDonald from 'C' company transferred to the new platoon. They did a lot of good work when the battalion went into action. They could drive any vehicle, fire all types of weapons and were experts in explosives. They were a hard bunch of men with very close camaraderie.

During this time the pipers had to learn First Aid and become stretcher-bearers. There were lectures from our Captain, a quiet religious officer who was later killed at the crossing of the Irrawaddy, a bullet passing through his helmet and killing him outright. The Padre, Captain MacLaughlan was on the same boat, but luckier, a bullet going through his helmet, but higher up and he never got a scratch. The last time I spoke to him long after the war he told me that he still had that helmet.

While we were at Visapur we were reinforced by men just out from Britain. Two of my pals from boyhood days were among them. Jimmy Brocken, who played the clarinet in the Military Band and Davy Reynolds, drummer, later killed at the battle of Hill 5120, part of the Kohima Campaign. It was at Visapur that we had a visit from Lord Louis Mountbatten. The battalion was rehearsed and drilled by Big Jim Haggart the Regimental Sergeant Major. Lord Louis arrived and he walked up to the saluting base, accepted the salute, then said 'gather round lads', then proceeded to give us the latest news about the war effort in Burma. There was no orderly drill movement as such this time and all the troops crowded in as close as possible to hear him talk.

Our main jungle training area was at a place called Belgaum which was about 100 miles south of Visapur. We would march out to the jungle, dig in and spend days in foxholes. While we were at one of these camps I had been teaching two young men to play the chanter, Paddy McCready from Northern Ireland and Norman MacDonald from Struan in Skye. They were ready to start on the bagpipes so I borrowed two sets of pipes, gave them the usual lecture on how to strike up the instrument and the value of the bag. I told them to go into a wooded area and practice, and also to learn to march to their music.

I left them alone to practice and went back fifteen minutes later but could not find them. It was not a thickly wooded area, but the trees were tall. I followed some footprints where they had scraped the leaves. It took me twenty minutes to find them. They had been playing a slow march My Home and were getting on well, but they could not turn round! I hadn't taught them that yet.

Norman was one of the early people wounded at Kohima and lost his hand. After the war, he worked in Singers, Clydebank with my brother.

Another Christmas and New Year were spent at one of these jungle camps. Whenever I think of some of these places there is always a little incident at the back of my mind. At such a camp I remember New Year's Eve and a beautiful singing voice in the distance singing The Bonnie Lass O' Ballochmyle, bringing home closer.

It was back to Ahmednagar and still more hard training. The straw huts with the dirt floors were becoming a luxury now after spending so much time in the open. I took ill at this time and could not eat. I was losing weight and had severe headaches so had to visit the Medical Officer. I had some sort of bowel infection and a fever, so I was kept in for a long time. My pals in the band used to come to visit me while I was hospitalised. While on one of these visits, in March, they told me that there was a move on. Some days after that we were told that the whole 2nd Division had moved up to Assam.

Chapter 11 – Over the Chindwin 1944 – 1945

Gradually we were getting snippets of news about the progress of the war against the Japanese, of the Camerons in action at Danapur, Kohima and the opening of the road to Imphal. The desperate fighting that these brave and well-trained men had gone through is well recorded in the Regimental history and various other books. Lord Louis Mountbatten said the Battle of Kohima was one of the greatest battles in history as it turned the tables for the Japanese in that area. They were turned back and kept on the run from then on. Any Cameron who fought at Kohima will tell the story of Hill 5120.

I began to improve in hospital and started to eat, so I was sent to a convalescent depot in Poona. I was there three weeks – the first week was relaxing but the second two weeks we did lots of physical training to harden us up for a return to our units.

It was back to Ahmednagar where I picked up my kit and joined a crowd of fellows who were also being drafted. So we travelled the long journey across India to join our battalion who were resting by this time at the 82nd milestone, right in the middle of North India.

It was good to get back to my pals again and there were a lot of new faces, unfortunately, a lot of absent ones too. Bobby MacFarlane, our lead drummer had been killed, Howard (Birdie) Lockhart had been wounded, Donald Stewart was wounded in the neck but never went to hospital. There were many stories to be told of those fierce four months battles.

Captain DJS Murray has to be remembered here, being a piper and having Snook Allan as platoon sergeant, both in the mortar platoon. They were experts in their job, as the Japanese found out to their cost. At one stage of the campaign, Captain Murray was Brigade Mortar Officer.

At the 82nd Milestone there was a hill on which the battalion was camped in shelters using the trees and tarpaulins. Tents were used for stores and Messes. The Engineers bulldozed the top of the hill away so we could have a sports field and football pitch.

Our Pipe Major, Norman Scott had been commissioned and went to the Graves Commission. Sergeant Allan left the Mortars Platoon and was appointed Pipe Major. However he was due a promotion to Colour Sergeant, so who could blame him, as his pay would be better. In those days a man appointed Pipe Major remained in the rank as Sergeant. After the war, that system was changed and 'a time served' promotion scheme was started.

The Battalion was having Highland Games and the Commanding Officer Lieutenant Colonel Somerville-McAlester (affectionately known as Sporran Jock) said to me

'I want you to compete on Saturday Macrae, and if you do well, I'll make you Pipe Major'

What a challenge to a man of 22 years age with only 6 years service.

There were entries from The Royal Scots, Kings Own Scottish Borderers and the Gordons. I had a successful day and was adjudged best piper of the day, Sammy Hall being the dancing champion of the competition.

That evening I was ordered to play in the Officer's Mess and had to include the tunes that I had played in the competition in my programme.

On Monday 23rd October 1944 I had to appear before the C.O. I was promoted to Lance Sergeant and appointed Pipe Major. Big Jim the RSM introduced me to the Sergeants Mess. It was a costly business – drinks all round!

Again the Battalion was preparing for a move so there was not much time for practice. However, we did manage to have massed bands with the 8th and 9th Gordons in Imphal. The RSM came with us and acted as Drum Major. It was a nice change and we made many friends in the Gordons. One man especially was Pipe Major Bob Slater of the 8th Gordons. We became great friends and he taught me the Football Song which became my party piece at Sergeant's Mess functions for years to come.

The 8th Gordons was an anti-tank regiment so their NCOs had gunner ranks. It was a Lance Bombardier Stewart of the 8th that composed the slow air The Heroes of Kohima, which I am glad to say has eventually found its way into published music.

During my stay at the 82nd Milestone, I had time to go and play at 33 Corps HQ. Again playing for General Christison and he never failed to come over and talk to the piper.

It was time to move again and we were to relieve the 11th East
African division. Being promoted to Pipe Major I was responsible to
the RSM for the battalion's supply of ammunition. The ammunition
was transported by mules until we arrived at the plains of Burma,
then we used vehicles driven by East African soldiers. A pontoon
bridge had been erected across the River Chindwin, where we
waited, I believe at Milestone 86 on the Imphal-Kohima road.

We had an early Christmas and New Year's celebration as we were
going to be in action on 25th December. I felt proud of having the
honour of playing my C.O. round the companies for the first time as
Pipe Major, where he wished them all a Happy New Year.

At this camp, I was sitting in a narrow trench writing letters to my
mother and Molly when a theme came into my head. I had no
manuscript but I designed my own on the writing pad and jotted
down some bars of music which kept running through my mind. I
kept humming it and playing it on the chanter. The next day the other
three parts fell into place. I had composed a tune. I carried it in my
pack until the war ended where we were stationed at Kamareddy.
Donald Stewart and Donald Matheson heard me playing it and
suggested we play it in the Officer's Mess. The idea was passed on
and the C.O. was to select a name. The suggestions made were
Colonel McAlester D.S.O, Sporran Jock or Over the Chindwin to
Mandalay. The Colonel selected Over the Chindwin.

We moved across the Chindwin and I was always with RSM Jim
Haggart. He was a fine man, always cheerful and kept everybody
going. We would be marching along and he would swing a pick-axe
shaft as if he were leading a band. He had been Drum Major at the

85

depot pre-war and had led the Massed Bands at the Empire Exhibition in Glasgow 1938.

There were skirmishes all the way but the Japanese were a beaten force and were now on the run.

When we got to Shwebo, just north of Mandalay, I was flown out to Chittagong to gather the pipes and drums kit.

I can tell this story now, but daren't tell it at the time or even during my army service.

I was in a transit camp at Chittagong and who should be there at the same time but Norman Scott. He came to my tent one evening and called me outside. He handed me some Officer's pips to put on my lapels then took me to the Officer's Mess and introduced me as Lieutenant Macrae. What a chance we both took, which still horrifies me to this day when I think about it. Maybe the last two years of training and living in the jungle was beginning to catch up with us, making us so reckless. I could have got detention and he could have been cashiered.

The band kit was for a triumphant march through Mandalay, but when we got there there were no streets to march through. However, the company pipers led their companies to the outskirts. I played for HQ Company and enjoyed it. We had special bags made for the pipes which were slung over our shoulders and easy to carry.

After Mandalay, I was sent on leave to Calcutta as a roster had been kept and I was due fourteen days. I didn't know it then, but I wasn't to return to Burma. However before we left the 82 Milestone I played at the unveiling of the War Memorial to the 2nd Division at Kohima, with the words we hear so often, *"When you go home tell them of us and say – for your tomorrow we gave our today"*

I also played at the unveiling of the Cameron Highlanders memorial stone on Hill 5120. I played Lochaber No More and the Naga tribesmen sang Onward Christian Soldiers at the service, in their own language.

Chapter 12 – The End of the Campaign 1945

Most of my leave was spent in the Sergeant's Mess and it was this leave camp we were told that the Battalion was being pulled out of Burma and were going to Bandel, a camp a few miles north of Calcutta.

The leave over, the Battalion all in camp, my job was to get the band together. It was then I realised I had a lot of friends, men who had other responsibilities but wanted to join the band. Dougald Smith from the Pioneers, Donald Stewart from General Reconnaissance, Jimmy Williamson from a duty company. Tam Hyde came back to the band, also Jock Laidlaw, whose pipes were always going and well looked after throughout the campaign. Sticky Kennedy volunteered to take the Tenor Drum, Paddy McCready though learning to play the pipes took the Bass Drum. We also had reinforcements from other regiments, one drummer from the RAF Regiment, Dursi Taylor who remained in the Camerons and left the regiment as a Company Sergeant Major.

One evening just as it was getting dusk I was playing my pipes, outside the band store, when I noticed a soldier with a side hat listening intently. When I finished he said in a highland voice 'That was good to listen to'. I asked him if he could play and offered him my pipes. He had a good finger and played some very musical pieces. He was Charlie Darroch Royal Engineers from Mull. In no time we had him transferred to the Camerons. He gave me a setting of the Liberton Pipe Band, a tune I'd never heard anyone else play, which he said he'd got from some old piper in Mull.

We soon had a pipe band knocked into shape and did a parade in Calcutta for a medal presentation. However, we had to look for a Drum Major as Big Jim was involved in his own job so it was given to Jock Godfrey a pre-war drummer but now in the M.T. Jock carried out the duties well until the war ended.

From Bandel, we moved west to Kamareddy, which is north of Secunderabad where we were earmarked for landings on Japanese held islands in the Indian Ocean. However, the dropping of the Atom Bomb on Hiroshima cancelled everything.

I remember sitting in the Sergeant's Mess at Kamareddy drinking with Sandy MacLean, Alex McQuade, Sheesh Gilles and Jock Godfrey when we heard the pipes, and we wondered what was going on. Word had got to the troops before the Sergeant's Mess and we were told the war was over!

I had a leave at the racecourse in Secunderabad, but there wasn't much to do but rest and listen to the stories in the Sergeant's Mess.

Donald Stewart had his wallet stolen by a Loose Wallah (from the Hindustani *Lus* for thief). He was raging and I was walking down the lines to the Sergeant's Mess for breakfast when the Canteen Boss came cycling through the lines. Any Indian would have got the edge of Donald's temper that morning. He chased after the Indian who dropped his bicycle and ran as he realised he could run faster than he could cycle. Donald could not catch him so he smashed the bicycle with a huge stone.

89

The celebrations went on for quite a while at Kamareddy, visits to the Officer's Mess, officers to the Sergeant's Mess and visits to the other ranks' canteen, which was called the 'Stagger In'

Willie Manson was the Officer's Mess Sergeant and we became great friends. We used to go out into the scrub for target practice. This was fun, then Willie suggested we collect frogs. We used to put them in our shirts and empty them on to the tables where the members were drinking. This was fun for a while, then Willie thought of a great idea – let's get a snake! We went out and caught a Krait, about eight inches long, one of the most poisonous snakes in India and put it in an empty gin bottle.

We walked into the Sergeant's Mess and turned the snake out onto the table. That shook the members and there was a mad rush for the tent opening. Another time he managed to get the poison out of the snake and hid it on his head under his bush hat. He frightened one of the officers in the mess this time. Willie was bald on top and when he took his hat off the snake remained curled up on his bald head.

I spent five days with Willie in his hotel Bayview House, Brora after the war and we had some fun, pipes and whisky for five days. His young son Benny (Benjamin Angus) was just starting to learn and I gave him a few lessons. He later joined us in Tripoli as National Serviceman and became an excellent player. From the 1st Battalion, he went to the 4/5th Camerons. When he finished his three years he emigrated to Canada and played with one of Canada's best pipe bands, the Powell River Pipe Band. Benny eventually settled in Dingwall.

The battalion was being sorted out to select men to go to Japan as occupation troops. Any soldier who had three years and eight months of service in India and Burma could get repatriation, but if he wished he could sign on for Japan.

I elected to go home as I wanted to get married and if I was to remain in the army as Pipe Major I would require a certificate.

All soldiers going home were posted to a transit camp at Kalyan outside Bombay. The camp Sergeant Major was Peter MacIntosh from Nairn, the man who had driven me from Richmond to Catterick Camp in 1938.

There was absolutely nothing to do in the camp as we were all waiting for the boat home. Again Sandy MacLean from Ross-Shire, Willie Manson from Brora, Sheesh Gilles from Fort William and I were great friends and we were joined by a Sergeant Major 'Jock' White DCM of the Worcestershire Regiment. He had a softy spot for the 'jocks' and he joined in all of our escapades.

The Mess would open and shut at the normal times, but we had a supply of Canadian beer hidden away for sessions during the hours the mess was closed.

Poor Peter MacIntosh was nearly driven mad with our antics and his words the day we left for Bombay and the troopship home were 'Thank God, you shower are leaving!'

I've met Peter a couple of times since those days when we've had a good laugh about it all and remained good friends.

It was November when we boarded the troopship Winchester Castle and took fourteen days to sail to Southampton – quite a change from the trip out.

Then followed a long train journey to Strathpeffer, with snow and wind on a cold winter night. The next day we were all documented and off on disembarkation leave for four weeks – two weeks in Stranraer and two weeks in Nairn.

The two weeks in Stranraer was fun and my father took a week's holiday which he was due. We used to get the bus to Stranraer and spend most of the day in the pub. I knew he was pleased that I had attained the rank of Pipe Major and I had to be in uniform everywhere we went. He would put on his best suit and hat, complete with Guards Brigade tie and walking stick. He had a slight limp from his Great War wound and was also slightly stooped from hard work. But when we used to walk out together, his shoulders went back, chest out – he was a different man on those days.

We would sit in the pub from opening to closing time and then shop around for 'a wee present for your mother'. A few more drams at five o'clock then a bus to Ardwell pub, which was nearer home, when we would spend the rest of the evening.

The 'present for your mother' was always a pan of different shape or size.

Years after my father passed away my mother used to talk about those peace offerings and laugh. She had more pans than she would ever use!

On the third week, I travelled up to Nairn to see Molly and her parents. We had a trip to Inverness for an engagement ring and plans to get married the following June 1946.

I returned to Hawick 11th Holding Battalion Stobs camp and an interview with Colonel Ronnie Miers who asked me if I was remaining in the army. I replied yes so he said

'Colonel Noble at the 5th Battalion is looking for a Pipe Major, do you want the job?'

I said I did and he asked the Adjutant if I'd had my end-war-leave. I didn't even know such a thing existed, so it was home for another week to Stranraer and a week in Nairn.

Again I returned to Stobs Camp for a week where I passed my time with the pipers. Ned Campbell MM Camerons was the Pipe Major. The Pipe Sergeant was Harry MacKenzie from Dingwall. It was a mixed band of Seaforths and Camerons.

Donnie MacPherson from Glenelg was a member of that band, who I later met up with occasionally.

It was with this band that I first met Ronnie Morrison from South Uist of the Lovat Scouts. An excellent piper, Ronnie had served in Greece and was waiting for his regiment after being home on compassionate leave. However, the war with the Japanese came to an end and he was being demobbed with his age group.

Talking with Ronnie later he recalled an incident one night when a terrific fight broke out between the Pipe Major and Pipe Sergeant.

Obviously, the two regiments were not yet ready for amalgamation in 1945.

So it was home again on disembarkation leave between Stranraer and Nairn and I made a mistake in the dates. I arrived back to camp one day late and was reported absent. I was marched in to face the music in front of a Major Fleming (Colonel Miers was away that day) who had been on leave at the same time in Nairn and I had passed him on the High Street. I'm glad I gave him a smart salute, as he was very lenient with me and accepted my story for being absent.

I was amazed at the amount of leave I'd had, maybe this was some sort of reward for all the hundreds of miles we had marched over India and Burma the last three years and eight months.

Chapter 13 – Victory Parades 1946 - 1947

I was issued with travel documents and off to Germany to join the 5th Battalion. It was a rough crossing from Harwich to the Hook-Of-Holland. Then a train journey to Bielefeld in Germany where I stayed for three days then on to Herrenhausen outside Hanover where the battalion was stationed.

I spent the next five months between Herrenhausen and Brussels, the latter being the place where the 5th Battalion was eventually disbanded.

The Battalion had a good little pipe band, Peter Sandilands, who originated from the 2nd Battalion was my Pipe Sergeant, James MacIntosh was the Pipe Corporal. Drum Major was Donald Fraser, known as Sharky, brother of Shug. We got on well together and had a lot of fun in Brussels during the gala season. We were invited to various parts of the city to lead the processions, entertain outside the main hall and play for a couple of Highland dances – Foursome Reel and Lochaber Broadswords. There would be a meal served and plenty of wine in the local hotel. The Drum Major always had a garland of flowers placed around his neck by the Gala Queen. He hated this and got ragged so much from the entire band.

It took quite a while for me to be accepted in the Sergeant's Mess as I was the only 'Burma Wallah' in the mess at that time. By the time we were about to be disbanded, I had been accepted and had made a lot of good friends. They must have realised that I was alright, just that I hadn't been in the same war as them. I knew they'd had a hard war and there were a few decorated members in the Mess.

There is a period I'll always remember of my short time with the 5th Camerons. It was during my visit to Wilhemshaven to say farewell to the 3 Cameron Highlanders of Ottawa, where we had plenty of fun but we were all very tired and liverish after three days celebration.

Arrangements were made for us to go to Verden to rehearse for the Victory Parade in London. There were bands from the 51st Highlanders and 52 Lowland Divisions. We were attached to the Gordon Highlanders and were well looked after. I'd been in massed bands just before the war and plenty after, but I'd never seen such a mass of pipers like this. Credit must go to the Drum Major of the Black Watch who got the drummers organised, the pipers properly drilled and all Drum Majors working together. The senior Pipe Major was Pipe Major Bunion, Kings Own Scottish Borderers.

I had a lot of fun with several Pipe Majors, John McKenzie, Argylls; George Wilson, Gordons; Charlie O'Brien, Seaforths; and Pipe Major Grey of the Scots Greys who had a brother, Lofty, in the Camerons before the war but who had left Aldershot early in 1939 to join the Police. He eventually moved to Illinois, USA. I met him at the Oban games in 1981 when he came over for a holiday. We had kept in touch and I was able to acquire a Cameron Tie and Regimental Badge for his blazer. I received a nice letter from him reminding me 'Once a Cameron, Always a Cameron'.

He was in the Edinburgh Police Force when I attended my Pipe Major's course in 1946/1947 under Pipe Major William Ross. We had some good nights together and he had a pass to visit the Castle Sergeant's Mess.

There were rehearsals every day and all day and we were in great shape for the Victory Day March in London. I remember one rehearsal at about five o'clock in the morning when I saw marching on the pavement beside the massed bands was Andrew MacIntosh from the Rose & Crown.

The Victory Parade went well as far as the massed bands were concerned and we then moved to Scotland to play in the main cities. A march along Princes Street, Edinburgh, then over to Glasgow to play at Hampden Park for the final of the Victory Cup between Rangers and Hibernian, which Rangers won 3-1.

After Glasgow, the 51st Division did the highland towns, the lowland division their own areas. Our first town was Aberdeen.

Arrangements had been made to get married in Nairn on 12th June but I was almost refused. I knew of a Major Harry Leah, a Cameron Highlander with whom I had an interview. I had no worries after that and my pay and warrant were arranged. I left Aberdeen on 11th June and got married in Nairn on 12th.

I then had to get the night train from Inverness that evening to join the bands in Perth for a show there on 13th. Next day, it was back up to Inverness for a march through the town and a show in Bught Park. I just had time to say hello to Molly and we were back to Queens Barracks, Perth and finally sent on leave for a belated honeymoon. Belated and short!

We were at Stranraer visiting my parents when I got a telegram to return to Brussels for an officer's farewell party and a trip to Paris. From that day on I realised that I was a soldier first and a married man second. Years later if I took a leave near barracks it would be granted with the words 'you'll have to come in and play at so and so'.

Molly never objected as she knew I enjoyed my job and realised what was required of me including loyalty to the regiment.

Preparations had been made for the 5th Battalion to be disbanded, so I applied for an interview with the Commanding Officer for a six-month course at Edinburgh Castle directed by Pipe Major William Ross. I had heard that the first course had started but my application was granted and I was at Edinburgh Castle from October 1946 to March 1947. My wife lived at Hamilton with her Aunt so I was able to go there and visit every weekend.

I worked hard on the course and enjoyed Willie Ross's teaching. I passed and received 'distinguished' report on my Pipe Major's certificate.

Chapter 14 – Life In Inverness 1947 - 1948

After the course, on returning to Inverness, I was informed that I was being posted to the 5th Scottish Parachute Battalion as Pipe Major. However the Depot Pipe Major, Ned Campbell took ill and was invalided out of the army, so the Commanding Officer Colonel Ronnie Miers told me I would remain at the Cameron Barracks and take over the band.

The Depot was then known as the 79 P.T.C (Personnel Training Centre).

I had a small band as most of the pipers were employed on other duties. However, there were a few boys to teach piping and dancing to, particularly Jock Smart who became a very fine highland dancer, George Riley and two young National Servicemen, John MacLeod from Portnalong, Skye and John Morrison from Stornoway.

When a band was required I could always get them together and rehearse for whatever engagement we had to do. The performances normally went well.

I was living with my in-laws in Nairn and travelled by bus to Inverness every day.

Micky MacKay had joined us at the 79th P.T.C and was my Pipe Sergeant. We were encouraged to go to as many highland games as possible by Colonel Miers. He would allow us transport but we had to be dressed in the full uniform of the Cameron Highlanders. The many games included Kingussie, Newtonmore, Glenurquhart and Strathpeffer, finishing the season at the Northern Meeting. Donald Stewart had married Shug Fraser's sister Annie and I would either spend the night with Donald or at Shug's mother's house. When I stayed the night at Donald's he would play the pipes at my room door on Sunday morning at half-past six!

While in Inverness I had to play in the Officer's Mess on guest nights and one night, in particular, I remember I'd finished and left the Mess in full kit, to catch the last bus to Nairn. While I was waiting at the bus stop Jack Murray, a Morayshire man, who worked in the Millburn Distillery, passed by and informed me that the last bus had gone, but there were plenty of fish wagons going from Ullapool to Aberdeen and I'd get a lift, no problem.

He invited me into the Distillery for a dram and a big and strong dram it was! I set off for Nairn with about two inches of snow on the ground. There wasn't a vehicle on the road that night and I walked all the way to Nairn, arriving at about five o'clock in the morning. I was none the worse but my buckle shoes suffered.

On the 30th August, I attended the Glenurquhart Games and had three seconds, one of them in the jig which I shared with Miss Edith MacPherson, who was taught by Willie Young. Edith was a good all-round player and had been well taught.

I got a lift on the British Legion bus to Inverness, then of course into the Legion bar for a drink. There was a piper Croachie MacKenzie from Nairn with me, so he had me play all the way to Nairn on the public bus. When I got to Nairn my father-in-law was waiting at the bus station. Grabbing my pipe box he said

'You'd better run home, she's waiting to go to hospital'.

I just had time to say hello and Molly went into hospital. What a Sunday morning I suffered waiting for Doctor MacDonald to come to the house and give us the news. Duncan my son was born at two o'clock on 31st August 1947.

The Inverness Piping Society used to meet at the Curling Club on Diriebught Road and we used to have some good nights. It was at one of those nights that a young boy John Allan was asked to play, but he didn't have a set of pipes. I let him play my pipes and I liked what I heard. I had him on my books as a future Cameron, but we lost him to the Scots Guards. However, he came to the amalgamated Seaforth/Camerons, The Queens Own Highlanders in 1962 as Pipe Major. He eventually became Major John Allan in charge of the Army School of Piping at Edinburgh Castle.

In February 1948 I was given my first married quarter at Fort George, only a few doors from Donald MacLeod Pipe Major of the Seaforth Highlanders who were also stationed at Fort George. Donald used to attend the Society Meetings and we travelled home to Fort George together. It was at one of these meetings that Sheriff Grant of Rothiemurchus asked me if I'd like to attend a piping course under John MacDonald. There was a course in progress at that time attended by Donald MacLeod, John MacLellan and John Garroway of the Glasgow Police

They used to practice what they'd been taught in the Cameron Barracks so I gleaned a lot of knowledge from them before I went to John MacDonald. I enjoyed his teachings and although he was seventy-nine years old and had stopped playing pipes he would demonstrate on the practice chanter and sing to us. Micky MacKay was also on the same course with us.

I used to go to Donald MacLeod's house at nights and we would sit around the fire and discuss what we had got from 'Johnnie' that day. Donald had got a lot more than I had from John and although I would be going to the games to compete against him the next day, he was always ready to give advice.

At one Kingussie games, I won the jig playing 'The Shaggy Grey Buck' and Donald came second. He congratulated me and said

'That's the first and last time you'll beat me Macrae'

And he was right.

We have been friends for many years since then and corresponded regularly. Donald went on to win everything going and had achieved eight clasps to his gold medal.

In June 1948 the 2nd Battalion came home to the Cameron Barracks and was disbanded. We marched them from the station to the barracks. Gus McNaughton was the Pipe Major and had successfully attended the same piping course as I had been on.

Chapter 15 – Presented to the King 1948 – 1949

The 1st Battalion arrived in Edinburgh April 1948 from the Far East after having served in Japan and Malaya. The 79th PTC was disbanding, so I was sent down with Drum Major 'Ginger' MacDonald to take over the 1st Battalion band.

On arrival at Redford Barracks, the Commanding Officer said to me

'I want you to get cracking and form a pipe band, as big as you can and as soon as possible, Oh by the way Captain Murray is the Pipe Band President'

Great I thought, a band president who knows what it is all about and wouldn't ask for the impossible.

I had plenty of pipers to choose from, pipers from 79th PTC, from the 2nd Battalion, and a mixed band from the Highland Brigade ITC (Infantry Training Centre). There were also pipers drafted in from other regiments. We could pick and choose who we wanted. We took Corporal John Margach, Jimmy Hughes, Shug Fraser, Alec Sandilands and John O'Rourke all from the Highland Brigade Band. Tam Pentland came as a Corporal with some of his drummers from the 5th Scottish Parachute Regiment Battalion.

It was hard work, plenty of kit and many sets of bagpipes but there weren't two chanters which matched. Corporal John Margach and I worked for hours scraping holes with tape trying to match as near as possible.

In two weeks we were able to present a band of twenty-four pipers, eight side drummers and a bass drum. John Margach was with me until he eventually retired in the 1950s.

What a loyal man he was and I could depend on him throughout the time we served together. I missed him when he left but he had set a good example for future NCOs in the band to live up to.

We played Retreats in the barracks and on the Castle Esplanade. Pipe Major William Ross thought we were so good that he arranged a broadcast for us which was done in the open air in Redford Barracks.

There were numerous guest nights in the Officer's Mess and one night Captain Murray asked me what piobaireachd I was going to play.

I said 'Mary's Praise, but I'll cut it short if you think it's too long' 'Certainly not', he replied, it's about time these people knew what it was all about'.

Captain John Sinclair fell asleep halfway through the tune, but being the gentleman he was, he came to the practice room the next morning and apologised to me.

During our stay in Redford Barracks, we had to return to Inverness with a contingent to take part in a Guard of Honour with the 4/5th Battalion for their Majesties King George VI, Queen Elizabeth and HRH Princess Margaret on the 24th June. The band played retreat in the late afternoon of the 25th in the barracks, at which their Majesties were present.

I was carrying the banner on my pipes which had previously been presented to the Battalion by King George V. When the performance was over I was presented to His Majesty by Colonel Duncan. His Majesty admired the banner and remarked that it was about time that he presented a banner to the regiment.

We were then posted to Bulford Barracks Salisbury, which was a cold place and not very exciting but we kept the band up to scratch and had a few engagements. At this time something got into my head that I'd like to join the police as my nine years were due to be up the next year in 1949. I applied but my application was turned down as I was a half-inch too short. Maybe if I'd told them I was a piper it

105

might have made a difference. I then decided to sign on for another three years.

It was while at Bulford that I had a visit from Jimmy Williamson who spent the night with us and we had some fun recalling our days in India and Burma. He worked in Swindon at that time.

Our wives had their Women's Guild organised by Mrs Duncan, the CO's wife and used to meet once a week. One night my wife came home and said

'The Battalion is going to Tripoli'.

The wives were told before the troops!

One good job we got to do was for a small band to play at the Chelsea Arts Ball in the Albert Hall. We were issued with old-time shell jackets and a bar of pipeclay to clean them. They looked good. It was an all-night party and there were some wild goings-on. I spent the night, or early hours, with a Lewis man, Campbell who had been a piper in the 2nd Camerons, years before the war.

I had to report to the CO when I returned and gave him a report on how the job went. I informed him that the pipers had played well. However, I think he wanted to know more, for his last remark before he dismissed me was 'I wish I was a piper'

In February 1949 the Battalion was sent on embarkation leave. Molly, Duncan and I had a cold journey to Stranraer. When we got to Port Logan, Molly and Duncan were very ill and had caught some sort of virus, which confined them to bed for most of the leave. The wooden rifle and sawmill-made toy wheelbarrow were there for the first grandson, which brought back memories. That was to be the last time my father saw Duncan, the boy who had been named after him and has grown as tall as his grandfather.

When I had to return to Bulford I had to leave Molly and Duncan behind as they were not fit to travel. They joined me at a later date but the illness had shaken them both.

Chapter 16 – North Africa and the first beard 1949-1951

The Battalion set sail for Tripoli in March on the ship Empire Trooper, leaving our families behind in Bulford Married Quarters until they joined us in July.

We were joining the Guards Brigade along with the Grenadier and Coldstream Guards. The Camerons were relieving the Irish Guards. A show was put on for both the bands of the Irish Guards and ours to play at.

Our main set included the tunes Leaving Glenurquhart, The Caledonian Canal and Over the Isles to America. This was the first time that I had met General Frank Richardson. He told me later that when he heard the Cameron band playing these tunes he couldn't believe his ears. Army pipe bands were changing with the times.

General Richardson and I became great friends through our love of Ceol Mor. He let me read his notes which he had kept when he would visit John MacDonald, which was an interesting book.

General Frank was ADMS in Tripoli (Assistant Director Medical Services) and one morning the Medical Sergeant told me I was wanted on the phone at the Medical Room, and to bring my chanter. It was the General and he wanted me to play the ground of MacDougal's Gathering.

I remember one occasion when Alec Peters (Big Eck as he was called) was in the hospital. The General was doing his rounds of inspections and saw Alec in bed. He sat down so long talking bagpipes that there was no time to finish his rounds. There was also a present of cigarettes for Alec.

The General was a funny man and you had to be quick to catch his humour. One time he was judging our annual piping competition. The band storeman came on to play and the General asked me what sort of player he was. I said

'a good band player but too fond of his bed!'

His reply was 'No harm in a piper being fond of his bed as long as he is in it by himself'

Another piper came on to play who had just got married in Tripoli, his bride having travelled out from Scotland. I informed the General about this and he asked 'Does his new wife like the pipe?'

When the Battalion went to Egypt in 1951 Molly and some of the pipers' wives were invited to tea at the General's home and entertained by Mrs Richardson.

Soldiering in Tripoli was pleasant but we still maintained a strong band. The pipers and drummers were involved in all military training and were mostly Battalion HQ Defence Platoon. We all enjoyed the training and we certainly covered quite a bit of desert. Sometimes we would play the part of the enemy and there was the time when half the band got lost in that role. They had marched too far off the maps they were using. Three days later they were found but were a tired and footsore bunch. They told the story about throwing their mess tins up in the air to attract the attention of a spotter plane. From then on whenever a plane flew over camp, wherever we were stationed, one senior NCO would shout 'Throw your mess tins at it!'

On the 8th June 1950, The Colour was trooped by the 1st Battalion Coldstream Guards. The pipers and drummers paraded with the Military Bands which consisted of the 4th/7th Royal Dragoon Guards and the Military Band of our own regiment. The only playing we had to do was to march the 1st Battalion Camerons on parade as they 'kept the ground' that day. My boyhood days came flooding back to me when the Military Bands played the tunes I remembered from my father's 78rpm record.

Our wives and families came out in July on one of the Empire Troopships. Some of the senior ranks walked up the gangways with bouquets. Molly asked me 'Where're my flowers?' In no way was I going to have it said that they saw the pipe major walking on board with a bunch of flowers!

We started to receive drafts of National Servicemen and if they could play the pipes or drums when they enlisted they were auditioned. If they were at the required standard, they were accepted into the band. From then numerous pipers passed through my hands. Too many to name here but as the years passed they could say 'I was in the Camerons with Pipie Macrae' and reflect it wasn't just Pipie Macrae who made the band, he had to have the good material to do it and the backing of his seniors.

On 23rd September 1950 Robina was born in the Military Hospital in Tripoli. We couldn't get an ambulance so Molly was transported to the hospital by the duty driver in a fifteen hundredweight wagon, propped up in the front seat with me sitting in the back.

While in Tripoli I received a telegram that my father was ill and unlikely to recover. I was flown home to London where I had to wait for the night train to Stranraer. I spent the day waiting in the Rose & Crown with Andrew MacIntosh and it was then he told me that he had worked with my father. From Stranraer I had to get a train to Ayr. Dad passed away half an hour after I got to Ballochmyle Hospital at the age of 65.

My parents had moved to a different house called Balkelly Cottage which was to be theirs for as long as they wanted to stay in it, but my father hadn't known that the house had been given to them. My mother lived in that house for twelve years after my father died until she was too old to live alone. The house is now derelict.

It was two months before I got back to Tripoli, waiting for a troopship

In 1951 we were flown to Egypt as trouble and skirmishes had started. I remember in the early hours of a cold morning waiting to board the plane, the Padre Captain Iverach MacDonald remarked about a 'rare morning for a drop of the craythur'. (Old expression for whisky) I told him there was a bottle in my pack. He asked 'What make?', when I told him it was an Irish he said 'Ach leave it where it is'

We arrived at Tel El Kebir, to a camp in the desert, but we had transport, not like the brave Cameron Highlanders who in 1882 marched all night with the Highland Brigade and into battle the next morning. We considered ourselves fit and hard but those highlanders must have been tough men.

There were skirmishes and casualties while we were in Tel El Kebir, which had been expected. The searchlights all around the perimeter had to be manned every night. No. 19 searchlight was the worst post as it was always getting shot at. The Egyptians would snipe at us from a building which was thought to have been a hospital or had been at one time. However Sergeant Arthur Smith ranged his 3-inch mortars on it, and when they started shooting again, the mortars opened up and there was no more sniping or hospital!

During our stay in Tel El Kebir, we were sitting in the Sergeants Mess tent discussing the water shortage, when the RSM said to the Pioneer Sergeant and me,

'I don't know what you two are worried about, you're allowed to grow beards'

Although we hadn't known it at the time this was a long-standing tradition in the British Army. Infantry pioneer warrant officers, colour sergeants, sergeants, drum and pipe majors have been permitted to wear full beards since late 19th century

Permission for us two to grow beards was granted the following day by the CO.

From Tel El Kebir we moved to Port Said where we were tasked with unloading the ships carrying military supplies, the Egyptian Dockers having been forced to turn against us. We were armed at all times on these jobs. One job I remember being on detail unloading mail from the passenger liner, en route for Australia. We were taken out on a barge to the ship. When the job was completed we set off on the barge back to base. Corporal George Johnstone played his pipes as we pulled away. All the passengers crowded the decks of the Liner and waved and cheered. George Johnstone from South Uist was the man who composed that well-known jig, Donella Beaton. He was a nephew of Pipe Major James Johnstone DCM, MM in the 1914-18 war. James Johnstone's bagpipes came to the regiment in 1959, thanks to David Murray. They were completely silver-mounted and I had the privilege of playing them until I left the battalion in 1961.

From Port Said we moved to Geneifa on the shore of the Great Bitter Lake (later renamed Kasfareet), again this was a tented camp. Things were a bit quieter here except for a two-day sandstorm where the sand blew into everything – your tent, food, kit. There was no escape! Some of the pipers even tried wearing gas-masks.

Captain Murray and I were invited to judge at a piping competition in Port Said, which the Scots Guards were organising. We were asked to bring along any Cameron pipers who would like to compete. We set off along the Canal road hoping to get to Port Said before dusk, but the vehicle we were in broke down. We were all well armed so Captain Murray placed all the pipers in position on either side of the road. We hi-jacked the first lorry that came along. It was an Egyptian lorry and the occupants were quite scared. However leaving Corporal Johnstone, with the driver and pipers we drove back about five miles to a R.E.M.E Recovery Unit, who immediately sent out an armed escort and Recovery Vehicle. I played the pipes in the R.E.M.E Officers Mess that night.

The Scots Guards were relieved to see us the next morning and the competition got underway. There were some good tunes. It was also nice meeting old friends again, Curly Roe, whose brother John was Pipe Major at that time and Pipe Sergeant Willie Strachan from Dundee. The leading drummer of the Scots Guards Band at that time was Sergeant Bill Williams, who I was to meet in later years when I was posted to the Liverpool Scottish.

Curly Roe was also a Pipe Sergeant. Jokingly I said to him 'Don't tell me you're going to compete', to which he replied 'of course'. I told him I was going to make faces at him while he was playing. However, while he was playing I kept my head down so as not to distract him, but happened to look up when he was nearly finished his reel which he had been playing beautifully! He burst out laughing and broke down. Curly got his own back on me in 1959 when I was stationed in Dover. I'd taken a contingent from my band to compete in a piping competition at the Drill Hall of the London Scottish in Buckingham Gate. The Sergeants Mess was three floors up and when I was playing my reel, Curly appeared on the veranda, outside, stuck his fingers to his nose and put his tongue out. I broke down, the score evened!

Our three years tour of the Middle East was over and we set sail from Port Said on the troopship HMT Lancashire, calling at Tripoli to pick up our families.

Chapter 17 – Back in Edinburgh 1951 - 1952

We eventually arrived in Edinburgh where we marched along Princes Street to a great welcome. Redford Barracks was to be our home for the next few months before going to Austria. Two days after arriving at Edinburgh I was asked to prepare the band for a BBC Studio recording, which was a success.

There were many other engagements organised for the band, also rehearsals for the Edinburgh Tattoo, which was becoming a big event by this time. The first official Edinburgh Military Tattoo was held in 1950.

There was to be a guard of honour for the Queen arriving in Edinburgh commanded by Captain T.B.M. Lamb and the Colours carried by Lieutenant Andrew Duncan. The BBC announced that the Cameron Band had twenty-five pipers on parade. Captain David Murray who was band president got a phone call from the famous John Morrison (jig John Morrison of Assynt House composed by Peter McLeod) asking if all the pipers were playing or were some just soldiers dressed to look like pipers. Captain Murray confirmed that they were all playing and not a twisted chanter on parade. In all my service I never had a dummy piper on parade. Not long after this Captain Murray received a box of kippers from John Morrison, which was shared out.

On the 27th June, the band played retreat at Holyrood Palace. We had twenty-four pipers on parade along with three bass and eight side drummers. Her Majesty Queen Elizabeth watched the show from the 1st-floor window accompanied by General Wimberley and she commanded us to do an encore after the retreat performance was over.

It was during our stay in Edinburgh that the young piper John D Burgess joined the regiment. John was a wonderful player, being a prodigy of Pipe Major Willie Ross. At the age of 17 in 1950 John won the Oban and Inverness Gold Medals. John was a favourite with the band and he was always respectful to me throughout his service. He attained the rank of Corporal and there wasn't a man in the regiment could say that John got his stripe just because he was a good piper. He worked hard at being a soldier and was always immaculately turned out. When he got his first stripe he carried out his duties with perfection so it was inevitable that the second stripe was on the way.

He was guided and kept right by Jimmy Hughes, who off parade was full of fun, but was a serious soldier when on parade and a proud Cameron. John D had signed on for three years but owing to circumstances beyond the regiment's control he left in 1955. He later joined the Edinburgh City Police and became pipe major of that band in 1957. Between 1962 and 1965, he was pipe major of the 4th/5th Battalion Cameron Highlanders TA Pipe Band.

26

Edinburgh's Bearded Piper

In all the British Army, only sergeants in the Pioneer Corps and pipers are allowed to wear beards. And the only beard in the Queen's Own Cameron Highlanders' band is worn by Pipe Major Mcrae who will draw crowds at the Edinburgh Festival next week

American tourist can't resist being photographed with the Pipe Major. Mcrae joined the Army as a boy in 1938, served in India, Germany, Tripoli and Suez

118

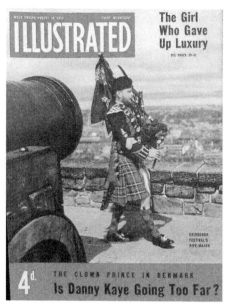

Unsigned painting found in Duke of Argyll Pub, London

The Tattoo finished, we were sent to Inverness, where we did an extensive tour of the Highlands – Nairn, Aviemore, Kingussie, Moy and Beauly. We then played over in the Western Isles – Portree, Broadford and Kyleakin. George MacKay who was the gamekeeper in Armadale when I was a boy came to see the band at Kyleakin.

119

Then we had a rough crossing to Lochmaddy in North Uist visiting Benbecula and then Lochboisdale in South Uist.

Chapter 18 – Stationed in Austria and Germany 1952 – 1954

T he tour over we left Inverness for Spittal in Austria. I enjoyed soldiering there and by this time we had quite a lot of men from the western isles, Willie MacKilloch from South Uist, Donald MacKinnon and Neil MacLeod from Harris. We also had one good player from Spean Bridge, Alec MacLeod. There were two brothers Steele in the band, one was a piper and the other a drummer. They were the sons of that great man who served in the Camerons, Pipe Major John Steele. It was said of him that he could throw the hammer, putting the shot, and pull in the tug-of-war, Highland dance and a great pipe player. He would win prizes at them all. I heard it remarked once that he was 'Steele by name and steel by nature'. He composed that beautiful tune The Hills of South Uist. I had the great pleasure of meeting him in 1952 when we went to South Uist.

We couldn't do many parades during the winter months in Austria, so everybody spent the days skiing on the hills. I used to put my skis on at the door of my married quarter, ski into barracks, call the roll and then off for the day. We still kept band practice going as we had a big programme ahead of us in 1953.

In July of that year 1953, we played at the White City Tattoo which was in aid of the charity S.S.A.F.A. (Soldiers, Sailors, Airmen and Families Association)

We were billeted in Chelsea Barracks and on arriving were warned by the Drum Major to be on the lookout for men in bowler hats carrying umbrellas and be sure to salute them as they were likely to be Guards Officers. One day the agent from a musical and drum instruments supplier called to see the Drum Major. He was a small man and remarked that the Cameron Highlanders were a very polite bunch of gentlemen. They had all given him a salute as he was wearing a bowler hat and carrying an umbrella.

There were the usual visits to the Rose & Crown Pub but Andrew MacIntosh had handed over to his son-in-law.

One lunchtime I was sitting with Drum Major MacDonald and some drummers and pipers when a gentleman walked in who looked familiar. The last time I had seen him was in the Northern Meeting Rooms in 1939. It was ex-RSM Robertson of the 2nd Battalion who had been commissioned just before war broke out. I approached him and he was delighted that a Cameron had recognised him. He sat down with us and we had a good long talk about the regiment.

He asked if we could meet him the next day at about the same time. We kept the appointment and during that chat, he gave me a beautiful silver cap badge. I was proud of that badge but unfortunately, it went missing on the troopship from Korea to Aden.

Her Majesty the Queen and the Duke of Edinburgh attended the White City Tattoo in aid of S.S.A.F.A. The ground was churned up by the horses and guns of K Battery. When the Royal car was leaving, the wheels got stuck in the mud. Corporal Hughes and I along with the Pipe Major of the Kings Own Scottish Borderers and his two NCOs were all in the front rank of the massed bands. We were beckoned to come forward and push the Royal car. Like one man we downed pipes, ran forward and pushed the car out of the mud. The Duke of Edinburgh called out 'Thank you gentlemen'

From Spittal, the military and pipe band went to Vienna for the Coronation parade along with a company of troops to take over the International Guard from the American Army. We were stationed in Schonbrunn Barracks. After a successful Coronation parade in the barracks, the band were engaged to visit the Russian Zone of Austria. The towns we visited were Wiener Neustadt, Eisenstadt, and Linz in the American Zone, where we were billeted in Camp McCauley. Then over the bridge across the Danube to Urfahr again in the Russian Zone. The last place we played at was St Polten, East of Linz where the crowd wouldn't disperse until we came out of the Town Hall to play again. It was in St Polten that the Burgomeister made a very forceful speech. When translated by the interpreter it came out as

'How nice it is to see some real soldiers, after being under our present guardians for the last eight years'.

While we were in Camp McCauley, the Americans didn't know what to make of us, we were dressed in KD shirts(khaki drill), kilt and spats. One of them even asked Piper Young if we were boy scouts.

All ranks used the same club. We were sitting passing the time, the Americans a bit shy of us and we were likewise. However, Jimmy Hughes knowing that the band was short of money and pooling what we had walked up to the Club Steward, saw on his shirt tag that his name was Smith and asked if he could call him 'Smiggy'. The next we saw, Jimmy was on the stage using the microphone doing his party piece, but slightly altered for an American audience, finishing his act by singing 'Dinah, is there anyone finer, in the state of Carolina'. I'd seen him do this act before but never in kilt and spats. Fortunately, there was no females present. When Jimmy came off the stage he received a terrific round of applause, with Jocks and Americans mixing, joking and laughing. Beer was being bought by the case!

We still had three towns to visit in the British Zone at the South of the country – Graz, Klagenfurt and Villach. The military band and highland dancers were with us and normally the pipes and dancers got the biggest ovation from the Austrian people, but on these three occasions, the military band stole the show. I guess because one of the tunes they played was the Radetzky March by Johann Strauss. During this tour, the officer in charge was Lieutenant John MacDonald son of the famous Colonel Jock MacDonald from Viewfield House, Portree.

Back to Spittal from Vienna and we started making arrangements for a trip home to Inverness to take part in the August 1953 Coronation Year Military Display. We were also appearing in this parade during which the Camerons would be given the Freedom of Inverness, along with Her Majesty the Queen Mother.

It was during this trip home that I was introduced to a young piper Andrew Venters. I found out what qualifications he had and told him he would be joining the band when he had finished his recruits training.

We had a leave, which I didn't enjoy, as my family were back in Austria and I had to remain in Scotland to take the military and pipe bands back to Austria. I spent my leave in Nairn sometimes going through to Inverness to visit old friends. One day while on leave I walked into a barbershop and asked him to take my beard off!

Returning to Inverness, my leave finished, I was walking through the barracks when I met Andrew Venters who I'd told that he could join the band when his training was finished. Approaching him I reminded him about coming to the band. His reply was

'Am nae comin' to your band, am gawn tae the man wi the baird'

I walked out in the evening to the Club Bar in Inverness and some of the west coast pipers were standing at the bar. Neil MacLeod was nearest the door so I greeted him in Gaelic, but he didn't recognise me. He had never seen me without the beard. Neil worked hard at his piping and became a good band player. One time he was entered for the novices boxing and was up against a young officer Lieutenant Rory MacDonald. They battled the three rounds to a standstill and were voted the best fight of the evening. Neil was taken in hand by Sergeant George Shannon and Sergeant Major MacNeil P.T. Instructor and father of the Celtic Football Team Manager Billy MacNeil. The following season Neil won all his fights within the distance. He eventually became a Headmaster at Kenmore, Loch Tay.

On returning to Austria, the CO sent for me to report on our visit to Inverness and he was displeased with me for removing my beard. I told a white lie, that I'd singed it with a cigarette lighter. General

Urquhart was visiting the battalion and we were formed up for inspection. He said to the CO 'I see you've got a new pipe major'

There was another incident with General Urquhart when four pipers and I were sent to play for the presentation of prizes for the skiing championships. We were watching the competition when the General came down the hill, and as he was slowing down, he fell. He could see we were amused.

A few weeks later he was visiting the regiment and the band were being taught to slalom by one of our Austrian instructors. I had about four flags to clear when I fell. The General saw this and laughed 'That's us quits Pipe Major!'

We were able to have a battalion piping competition at Spittal and Major Archie MacNab, who had been in the 2nd Battalion during the war and now working with the Italian Police, travelled from Italy to adjudicate. We had a successful competition and a band Ceilidh in the evening.

Next day was Sunday and Archie arrived at my home where we had the pipes going all day. I'd heard a lot about Archie MacNab and his playing, but to hear him play for a whole day, with the occasional break for refreshments, was something I'll never forget. I met him many times in 1960 while stationed in Edinburgh, but never heard him play again.

It was now time to leave Austria to complete our three years tour in Luneburg, Germany. Again our families were sent ahead of us, so it was farewell to Spittal in November 1953.

126

At Luneburg normal training carried on with occasional retreats and guest nights in the Officer's Mess for the pipers. There used to be patrolling along the villages between West and East Germany, so the pipers were always in demand to accompany them.

At first, we were stationed in Wyvern Barracks but were later moved to the Airfield. I had three good pipers join us in Wyvern Barracks, Duncan MacDonald from Skye, Alec Shand and Eddie Pinkman from Edinburgh.

We had a visit from the Duke of Edinburgh while we were stationed at the Airfield. He was our Colonel-in-Chief and when he stepped off the aeroplane, which it was rumoured he'd piloted himself, he was dressed as a Cameron Highlander. He was also Colonel-in-Chief of the 8th Hussars who were stationed in Wyvern Barracks, so he left Luneburg in their uniform.

I was now Colour Sergeant, appointed Pipe Major. In 1949 an order had been issued that Pipe Majors, Drum Majors after the rank of Sergeant for three years would be promoted to Colour Sergeant. I automatically went up one rank after being a Sergeant since 1944. I was now due promotion to Warrant Officer on 12th October 1954.

So I was taken off all band duties and went back to school for intensive education to prepare for an exam for my 1st Class Education Certificate, which one had to have before being promoted to Warrant Officer. The subjects studied were current affairs, map reading, geography, maths and English. However, I successfully passed the exam and was duly promoted to Warrant Officer, still with the appointment of Pipe Major. This way Commanding Officers

127

could retain their Pipe Majors longer, not having to leave the band seeking promotion.

I must mention here my next-door neighbour in married quarters, Sergeant George Shannon, who had joined the regiment at the 82 Milestone in Assam during the war, transferred from the Royal Artillery but became a staunch Cameron. He had a good head for maths and while preparing for my exam I used to go to his house every evening and he would help me with problems and how to simplify them. At first appearance, you couldn't think of George as having a brilliant brain, but inwardly he was a clever man. He was also a clever boxer and when we were stationed in Assam, he and Irishman Paddy Cullen used to give black and white demonstrations to the various regiments. Paddy's fiancée came from Liverpool and he had Maggie May painted on the butt of his Bren gun throughout the campaign in Burma.

George loved playing the mouth organ and knew all the pipe band tunes. We were having a bottle of beer in the Sergeants Mess in Austria and he said 'I've composed a pipe tune' and played it to me. It was a fine going march so I wrote it down on a piece of manuscript. I asked him what he was going to call it and he said Strains of Villacher. Villacher was the beer we used to drink in the mess, a strong brew but good beer. I had the manuscript for a long time, but at some time went astray. Had I still got it, no doubt it would have found its way into some music book?

I visited Paddy Cullen in later years in Liverpool. He was from Wexford but had married and worked in the Post Office in Liverpool. He used to joke about his house is next door to the Orange Lodge.

128

National Servicemen were still joining and we were still getting good pipers. Two players with a good piobaireachd grounding, taught by J. P. Grant of Rothiemurchus, (the 'Sheriff' of piping folklore), were John Stewart from Aviemore and Ian Fraser from Carrbridge. If Ian was ever asked where he got a setting of a tune from he always answered 'The Sheriff'. Ian got the nickname Sheriff and was still referred to by that name as long as I know. I still met up with these men for many years and we always had some good laughs. John Stewart joined the Aberdeen Police, becoming a Sergeant. He was very kind to me when I was hospitalised in Aberdeen.

Andrew MacCormack joined us about the same time. He came from Dufftown and had some funny expressions. He was on a route march with John Stewart on a cold winter's day and when asked how he felt on returning to barracks, he said in his East coast accent

'Ma lugs are like tattie crisps!'

Another time when we were rehearsing with the military band for some ceremonial parade, Andy was heard to remark

'That ither band sounds like some bugger washing dishes'

On one occasion when the band was on leave, there were a few pipers left in barracks with Corporal John D Burgess in charge. He was asked to detail a piper for a route march and he selected John Stewart. Poor John, he hadn't been long in the band and didn't have a great selection of route march tunes, so he set off at the head of the company playing Balmoral Highlanders at the tempo he had been taught for competition. The troops had never been taught to march at this slow pace and they were in a shambles. John was sent back to

129

barracks, but it didn't take him long to learn and make his own contribution to the band that was expected of him.

Again, home to Edinburgh for another Military Tattoo. There were many rehearsals and then the actual show. We were attached to the Royal Artillery in Redford Barracks. All the Pipe and Drum Majors in one room. We used to lie in till mid-day as there was little to do before the Tattoo got underway. One morning the Gunner's Orderly Officer put his head in the door and asked who was in charge of this barrack room. Donald MacInnes of the KOSB called out 'Pipe Major Willie Ross!' The Orderly Officer told his Sergeant Major to make a note of that. Pipe Major Ross heard the story and enjoyed the funny side of it – He was seventy-five at the time.

The Tattoo ended and we returned to Luneburg.

Chapter 19 - Introduced to Her Majesty 1955

The next move was to be to Elgin. We were to parade at the Ceremony of the Keys in Edinburgh. This is when the Queen is welcomed into the city of Edinburgh, 'your ancient and hereditary kingdom of Scotland' by the Lord Provost, who offers her the keys of the city. We would also parade for the Presentation of Colours by Her Majesty at Balmoral.

It was becoming a habit now, families being packed off home before the battalion. We left Luneburg on a cold winter morning and arrived forty hours later to an even colder night in Pinefield Camp, Elgin, with no water supply, and everything froze over. It took a few days to get the camp and family quarters organised.

We had the normal regimental duties and drills with much practice for the Colour Presentation

The BBC had made arrangements to do a recording on a Saturday morning for a regimental programme. The recording was done in the open air but I had good players and the recordings were excellent.

There was a rail strike at this time in 1955 and we had to travel by road to Edinburgh for the installation of General Sir Horatius Murray (a distinguished former Cameron Highlander) as Governor of Edinburgh Castle

On the 6th June, we were at Balmoral Castle for the Presentation of the Colours. The Battalion and bands were well-rehearsed for this historical parade which went off without a hitch and the weather was beautiful. When the parade was over I had to play at the garden party, wearing on my pipes the Banner presented to the regiment by our Colonel-in-Chief HRH the Duke of Edinburgh.

I was in the staff quarters taking the banner off my pipes and just about to leave when the adjutant Major Sun MC came in and said

'Don't go yet Pipe Major, Her Majesty wants to talk to you'.

Her Majesty duly arrived accompanied by the Duke of Edinburgh. I was presented to them and the Duke of Edinburgh asked

'Were you one of the men that pushed our car out of the mud at the White City Tattoo?'

I replied that I was and the Queen remarked 'But you had a beard then'

Chapter 20 – Posted To Korea and Aden 1955 - 1958

The Battalion should have sailed from Southampton but because of the rail strike, the troopship Dunera was brought to Clydebank. However, for some reason, a train was then available to take us from Elgin to Glasgow and we set sail for Korea on 23rd June 1955.

There was a refuelling stop at Malta and on the way through the Suez Canal, we were told to watch out on the starboard side. There we saw the pipes and drums of the Royal Scots playing us through that part of the canal with Shug Fraser as their Pipe Major.

The next stop was Aden where we were granted shore leave with a chance to stretch our legs.

On again with a stop at Colombo but no shore leave this time.

It was about this time that Colonel W.A. Stevenson permitted the Pioneer Sergeant and me that if we wished we could grow back our beards. It took a couple of weeks before they looked anything like beards but by the time we landed at Incheon in South Korea they looked in good shape.

The Pipes and Drums played on the quayside and then the Ghurkhas band entertained us.

Shore leave was granted and everybody had to be back on board by a specific time. Duncan MacDonald and Alec Shand were late and were spotted by the Military Police. They managed to avoid them as far as the dock and they arrived at the dockside at the same time as the police jeep.

Some families were going on board, en route to Hong Kong. Duncan and Alec took their hats off and put them in the pram and got on board undetected carrying the pram.

We were in a transit camp at Incheon for a few days before moving up to our camp at Munsa-an-ni where we were to relieve the 1st Battalion Dorset Regiment. The first thing that caught one's eye was a signpost in the middle of the camp which read Inverness 5200 miles. It wasn't a very exciting place to be, surrounded by scrubland hills and that mountain Gamaksan which caught your eye every time you walked through the camp. Again one wondered why brave men had to give their lives for a place like this. It was one station which I never enjoyed but just had to get on with it.

As always when we were stationed in inhospitable places the band developed special characters.

Eddie Pinkman was one of these men who had served in the Royal Scots at one time. He was a clever musician, he could play the accordion, clarinet, guitar, piano and was also an excellent piper. Eddie was well known to be fond of a dram, but the person who got into bother through his drinking was himself and he never harmed anyone.

I was playing at a guest night in the Officer's Mess with Duncan MacDonald and Eddie. Our programme was over; Major Beaton came over to congratulate us on our performance and asked me what

I would like to drink. I said I'd like a whisky. He said to the Mess Sergeant

'A double whisky for the Pipe Major, what would you like MacDonald?' 'The same as the Pipe Major Sir' answered Duncan. 'What about you Pinkman?'

Eddie had a stutter which he used to laugh about himself. He tried to say what he wanted when two bottles of beer fell out of his plaid.

'Pinkman' shouted the Major, 'you were pinching the Officer's Mess beer, for that, you're not getting anything'

On the way back to our billets I heard Eddie say to Duncan

'He can k-k-k-keep his dram, I've got a b-b-b-bottle in ma kitbag'

There used to be a lot of night guard as thieves known as slicky boys would break into camp to steal, plus the fact that we were situated so near to the DMZ (Demilitarised Zone). All sentries were issued with live ammunition.

I was duty Warrant Officer one Sunday morning and Lieutenant D.A.N.C Miers was the Orderly Officer. Reveille was at 6.30 am and time to inspect the night guards and ensure they had all been relieved of their ammunition. It was the duty piper's first duty of the day to play reveille but this morning there was no piper. Lieutenant Miers wanted to know which piper should have been on duty and I went to the pipers' hut to see who should have been on. It was Eddie Pinkman. I went to his bed and saw that it had not been slept in.

On my way back to report to the Orderly Officer, there was Pinkman, coming over the hill, dishevelled, soaking wet. I called his name and he replied

'It's a-a-a-alright, a-a-a-a'll put myself in' and marched into the guardroom.

Allan Roscoe, six foot four, was a good operatic singer and was always in demand to sing at the American camps.

Andy MacCormack, who I've mentioned earlier in Austria was also a fiddle player. The Battalion formed its own Scottish Dance Band, so Eddie Pinkman and Andy played in it. Like Allan Roscoe, they were always in demand.

We now had Drum Major George Burns, as Drum Major MacDonald had taken ill at the 1954 Tattoo and was unfit to go to Korea.

We worked hard at band practice, always learning new tunes and we reached a standard I was pleased with.

During the winter all units had their annual administrative inspection. We were the only band out there so we had to play for the parades of the Canadians, Kiwis, Australians, Royal Artillery, Engineers and Captain Hickey of the Army Air Corps. He had about twenty men in his unit and they flew spotter aircraft.

Captain Hickey took me for a flight one day over the DMZ and pointed out the North Korean positions, then over our camp flying over the Sergeants Mess.

137

On all these parades the troops were dressed in complete winter kit but the pipers and drummers had to be in kilt. Our only consolation was we were allowed to wear mittens, except when playing of course.

During our year or more in Korea, the band paid a visit to Japan, where we played in Kure, Hiroshima. We also played at the Tokyo Officer's Open Mess for high-ranking diplomatic and military personnel in the Far East. These performances were to last two weeks then two weeks leave in Ebisu Camp, Tokyo.

Lieutenant Donald MacLean from North Uist was with us by this time and I had some laughs with him during our stay in Japan. There was also a boat trip to Iwakuni to play Retreat.

My visit to Japan was cut short as there had been a dreadful fire in one of the Sergeants' mess huts. Four senior NCOs had lost their lives and I was required to play the laments at their military funeral in Pusan, South Korea.

There were no other passengers on the Dakota that flew Corporal Miller and me back to Korea and as I'd met the pilot the previous night, he invited me to sit beside him upfront during the flight. The scenery was impressive from that seat in the aeroplane, looking out without straining one's neck.

It was a sad return to Korea and I didn't know who had lost their lives until I returned to camp. We had all been good friends. Fire precautions became very strict from then onwards.

The Battalion was invited to celebrate the 1956 4th of July
Independence Day by marching through Seoul, the capital of Korea.
It was an impressive parade and we were well entertained when the
parade was over. We made lots of friends from the American 21st
Infantry Regiment. One man I especially remember was Top
Sergeant Upton. He arrived at my band store on one occasion, 'Here
you are Evan, a present for your boys' He had cartons of fresh milk
in the jeep trailer.

Two pipers had the opportunity of going to Seoul where they met a
Major John McEwing US Airforce. He asked them who their Pipe
Major was and when they told him he said

'Ask him to send me a couple of reeds'.

I never did, but one day walking through camp I met our Colonel
with Major McEwing. I was introduced to him and as I remembered
the reeds my words were 'They're no good without the chanter'.

Many years later from 1975 onwards I'd get a Christmas card from
John McEwing never making the connection and thought it was
somebody taking a piper's name off a Northern Meetings
programme. But in February 1980 a letter arrived from Spokane,
Washington. It was from John inviting me to come out and teach at
his Piping School in Coeur d'Alene for two weeks in July, which he
had founded and organised for over eight years. Poor John, I was just
getting to know him, but at the end of the first week, he had a heart
attack. I visited him in the hospital before I came home. I received a
letter from him after he came out of hospital, but he passed away in

November. I liked John very much and his hobby was the College and how much he could do for piping.

Every time I met him, the few times they were, he would say 'It's no good without a chanter!'

Jimmy Hughes was a Sergeant by this time but was sent home on compassionate leave, his son had had an accident and lost an eye. He arrived back out bringing some new recruits with him.

We didn't get mail every day and there would be a sign on the Sergeant's Mess bar 'Mail Delayed 24 hours' (or 48 hours) whichever the time might be.

We had a Corporal in the Signal Platoon who had written to a Scottish piper and signed it, "lonely soldier in Korea". He received more mail than he was ever able to read. When a 'mail delayed' notice appeared on the bar, Jimmy would get a bag of mail from the Signals Corporal and put five or six letters in everybody's rack, from the RSM to the youngest Sergeant. This cheered everybody up!

It was nearing time to leave Korea and it was rumoured we were going to Hong Kong, but that move was cancelled and the advance party was sent to Malaya.

We boarded the Empire Orwell to a farewell from our American friends, then we were told that we were going to Aden, as trouble had started in the Suez Canal Zone and British troops had landed in Egypt.

A hot tented camp was our reception at Aden and the Battalion was split up. HQ was at Singapore Lines, 'A' Company at Little Aden, 'C' Company at Steamer Point and 'B' Company were up country at Dhala (or Ad Dali). 'D' Company was based at RAF Khormakser and then on to the Yemen border at Mukayris. Every company had its own pipers so the band was slightly depleted in numbers. However, we had some new pipers join us later.

Barracks were being built for us, but in the meantime, the members of the Sergeants Mess were using the mess of the Aden Protectorate Levies (APL). This was an Arab military force created for the local defence of the *Aden Protectorate* under British rule. The *Levies* were drawn from all parts of the *Protectorate* and were armed and officered by the British military.

A Piping Competition was arranged for the Battalion pipers in Aden judged by Padre Joe Brown and myself. The pipers had become friendly with an RAF man from Islay, Angus Currie and a good piper. He was allowed to take part in the open competition.

Many years later I met him in Oban at the games where his son was competing in the juvenile competitions. He came up to me, shook hands and produced the medal he'd won in Aden.

Soldiering still had to go on and the band was employed to escort the supply convoys through the desert and across mountain passes to Dhala.

It was at Dhala that big Joe Murray was wounded. Joe had joined the Seaforths but transferred to the Camerons after the war. He had been in the band in Bulford and Tripoli but left to get a promotion. Joe was a hard man but never got over his wound and always had that telltale limp.

Piper McCourt was badly wounded when he was leading 'B' Company, commanded by Major Christopher Grant. They had run into an ambush. He was lame for a long time but when I saw him eventually in 1976 he seemed to have got over it. His son joined the Queens Own Highlanders as a piper in 1979.

Molly, Duncan and Robina arrived out in Aden along with some other families and I had got a married quarter in the Crater district. Molly wasn't very fond of the area, but one couldn't pick and choose. She and the children had been in family quarters in Berwick while we were stationed in Korea. The children loved the heat and there was plenty of swimming.

I was appointed a Somali boy to help with the shopping as the Arabs weren't very polite to British females if they were unescorted..

One day Molly told Omar to go and buy a turkey for Christmas and to pluck it. She advised him to dip it in hot water as it would be easier to get the feathers off. But she forgot to tell him to have it killed first. He brought home a live chicken, which he despatched behind the apartments.

I met a gentleman from Dundee who invited me to his house and to bring some pipers with me and an accordion player.

His wife explained that their budgie was fond of music and would sing when the music started. Every time Eddie Pinkman struck up the accordion the budgerigar screamed. In the end and after a few drams

142

Eddie could stand it no more and said 'Yer b-b-b-bloody budgie can sing nane'.

It was time to go back to camp.

Colonel P.M. Hunt took over the Battalion in Aden. We now had our barracks built in Singapore Lines and we had our own Sergeants Mess.

It was in this Sergeants Mess that we were summoned to be told that the regiment was going to amalgamate with the Seaforth Highlanders in 1961. There were some sad faces in the mess that night. Men who had fought in the desert, Burma, Italy, France and Germany almost in tears at the thought of their regiment with its historic past being amalgamated.

Chapter 21 – Home to Dover and Edinburgh 1958 - 1961

The morning came when we were to leave Aden. The Troopship Devonshire was in port waiting to take us home to the UK. The children were sent off to school as normal that morning and Molly was to hand the house over to the incoming regiment. I was on parade with the Battalion. When the children eventually got home from school, Duncan said to me 'You owe me ten shillings, Dad'. He had passed his eleven plus. I'd forgotten about this but I had told him in one of my weaker moments that if he did well at school, ten shillings(50p) would be his reward.

We had a pleasant journey home on the Devonshire, with the best of treatment. Baby sitters and child minders were organised by the shipping line to look after the children, while the husbands and wives enjoyed a luxurious cruise.

We arrived at Liverpool docks on 9th April 1958 with the band of the Liverpool Scottish welcoming us home to the tune The Cameron Men. Also waiting to wish the battalion a welcome home were Lochiel (Chief of the Clan Cameron), General Douglas Wimberley, General Sir Colin Barber and Provost Robert Wotherspoon from Inverness.

Our families were sent to their respective homes and we were to follow them on leave at a later date.

We boarded the troop train for Dover, appropriately named Cameron Highlander. A couple of days at Dover and most of the battalion boarded a special train for London and from there we all went our various ways.

Sergeant George Shannon and I were travelling to Inverness and we were fortunate to book sleepers. We had an hour to wait before the train departed from Kings Cross so we decided to go to the bar for a drink. Sergeant Shannon was wearing uniform and I was in civilian clothes. There was a gentleman in the bar who asked George if he'd just returned from Aden. When he told him he had, the gentleman said 'have a whisky'. George said 'this is the Pipe Major' introducing me, so the gentleman said 'give him a double!'

In the evening on the train, the attendant delivered four miniature whiskies and another two with our morning tea, all with the compliments of Provost Robert Wotherspoon. A Provost proud of his county regiment.

After our leave, we returned to Dover, unpacked our kit and made preparations for training at East Wretham Camp in Norfolk. The band had also been booked to play at the Edinburgh Tattoo. The battalion went off to East Wretham and the band was fully involved in the training. All the pipers were assigned to their own companies.

Two pipers were required to board the Royal Yacht Britannia at Immingham Docks, Grimsby. They were going to be entertaining the Royal Family while the yacht sailed up the east coast to Dundee. The two pipers selected were Hamish Hamilton and George MacKendrick. Not long after Hamish came back from the Royal trip he was posted to Inverness Depot as a Training Corporal. He was a fine soldier, a good piper and a loss to the band. He eventually became a history teacher in Aberdeen.

While at East Wretham the CO sent for me and asked

'How would you like a trip to Inverness for a few weeks? Major Murray is in charge of the depot and thought it would be a good idea if you were up there, to go round the games competing with two young pipers who have just enlisted'.

Back to Dover and then off to Inverness.

The two young pipers were Ian MacFadyen and John MacDougall. Ian had already won the Gold Medal in 1957 and John was to win it in 1960. Two fine young men and we were to get on well from the start and I enjoyed their company. I didn't enjoy the games that year as I'd been so long away from competition and suffered terribly with nerves. However, John and Ian were always sure to be on the prize list.

The depot had a small band at this time which played for drill parades when required. John and Ian were part of this band; Joe Murray was Provost Sergeant and took the bass drum on these parades.

On one occasion when the troops were formed-up on parade ready for inspection, the company was told to fall out and be ready to continue in twenty minutes. While they were waiting RSM Smith told Ian MacFadyen to play a tune. Ian said 'what tune should I play?' Joe Murray shouted 'The Campbells are coming!'

Major DJS Murray came out of the Officer's Mess and ordered the piper marched to the guardroom. However he wasn't in the guardroom for long and there were no charges made, just a lecture about the Camerons never played that tune - ever.

Ian was walking out that evening past the Officer's Mess when he heard someone whistling The Campbells are Coming. Looking up at the window he saw Major Murray.

We attended the Oban Games that year and were worried that as we were dressed as Cameron Highlanders the massed bands would march to the field playing The Campbells are Coming. We agreed we would join in when the tune changed to the Argyllshire Gathering. Later, a local paper received a letter from a spectator who was amazed that some pipers didn't know one of the tunes. One was even a Pipe Major in a famous Highland Regiment.

I had a trip to Skye with the City of Wellington Pipe Band from New Zealand. A great bunch of fellows and I hadn't realised until then how piping was being kept alive over there. They were all fine players.

Due to my travelling back and fore I missed the Edinburgh Tattoo that year but the band came to Inverness after the Tattoo was finished.

1959 was to be a busy year for the band. Our families were stationed in Dover and on 23rd May the band was sent to Portugal to play in Oporto. The band was well entertained and every member was presented with a medal.

From there we went to Lisbon where we were to rehearse for a tattoo. We were stationed in Police Barracks. The troops weren't too happy, but they had one consolation, they received two free bottles of beer each day. We met up with old friends and we used to have good fun. The RSM of the Coldstream Guards was an old friend from Tripoli days, and Pipe Major Robert Crabb of the Scots Guards who I used to have a lot of fun with.

There was a young Scots Guards Corporal on that Tattoo, who could be heard practicing every morning early, on the practice chanter. I didn't know him so well then but got to know him later and it wasn't long before he made his mark in the piping world. He became Pipe Major W.O.1 Angus MacDonald at the Army School of Piping.

Home from Lisbon and we were off again for a week in Guernsey to play at various engagements. The band was a lot happier on this job as I think their food was better.

I accompanied the dancing team in a performance for HRH Princess Margaret.

By this time we had acquired a good piper and expert dancer Ian MacDonald known as MacDonald 66. As we had six MacDonalds in the band at one time we usually put two figures after their names. MacDonald 45 was the brother of Rhona MacDonald one of Scotland's greatest lady players and the first lady to win a prize at the Northern Meetings. I had the occasion of meeting her father Archie who had served in the Lovat Scouts and Camerons. I spent an afternoon with him when we visited South Uist. He was a great character, typical of the highland piper who knew all the stories.

148

On our return from Guernsey, we had to go to take part in the film 'Make Mine A Million' with Arthur Askey and Sid James. This too was good fun.

During one lunch Captain MacKinnon, who was band president at that time met Laurence Harvey, who was on another set with French actress Simone Signoret, making Room At The Top. She had been making a fuss about something and I think Laurence Harvey was getting fed up with it. After we had done our part, it was arranged that when the cameras started rolling on the other set, we would march through the whole show. We formed up at the hangar door and at a signal from Laurence Harvey we marched in and disrupted the film-making. Thankfully it went down well and there was no offence taken.

Once more July was busy with a return to the Highlands and a visit to North and South Uist, which would be the last time as Queens Own Cameron Highlanders. There we had another chance to catch up with old acquaintances and have some fun. We said goodbye to Lochboisdale and took the boat to Mallaig and the long journey by train to London. It was while passing through Fort William that I received a parcel of kippers addressed to the Pipe Major. At the time I didn't know where they had come from but found out later in 1974 when I eventually went to live in Fort William that they were left for me by Alec MacDonald who had been the Station Master.

It was a tired and weary band that got off the train in London but not to return to Dover yet. We had to board a bus and go to Woburn Abbey to play at a garden fete. However, as usual, the band rose to the occasion and put on a spectacular show after which we were received and refreshed by the Duke and Duchess of Bedford.

Returning to Dover, there wasn't much time to prepare for the next Edinburgh Tattoo (1959), but there were the usual tunes to learn for the massed bands, which was always a success at the tattoo. There were no other engagements while we were in Edinburgh so I was glad when the tattoo was over and we returned to Dover, as there was a baby due in September.

A couple of days before the baby was due to arrive I was given two weeks leave and Lorraine was born at home on 2nd of September. I kept house and did all the necessary chores and had my leg pulled by the other soldiers' wives about my wonderful whites on the line. It is amazing how one copes with these jobs when it is necessary.

We spent a cold Christmas in Dover but were told that we were to tour the United States in 1960 after another Edinburgh Tattoo.

The Battalion moved to Redford Barracks, Edinburgh in January where we moved into married quarters and would remain there before amalgamation with the Seaforth Highlanders.

Meanwhile, there was a British Trades Fair in New York in June with a Tattoo in Madison Square Garden. There was a dinner in the Waldorf Astoria for the English Speaking Union in honour of HRH Prince Philip, Duke of Edinburgh. I took four dancers over and we were billeted on Governor's Island. We played at the dinner on 9th June and on the 10th we were formed up as a Guard of Honour at the Trades Fair opening. The Duke came over and spoke to me introducing me to President Nixon as Pipe Major of his regiment.

I had to fly back the next day but left the dancers there to take part in the Tattoo. On the way home I had to deliver the Duke's Pipe Banner to Buckingham Palace which I had displayed on my pipes at the dinner, in New York.

There were lots of parades for the band in Edinburgh: guard mounting at the Castle, also the guard at Holyrood Palace which always drew a huge crowd. I enjoyed the march from the Castle to Holyrood Palace as there was always an ex-Cameron in the crowd who would call out to me as we marched along the street.

Tattoo rehearsal had started and we now had Tam Pentland as Drum Major. We got on well and had the band in good shape for the Tattoo and the forthcoming tour of America.

The Regiment also rehearsed for the Tattoo and one of the items was the 2nd Battalion Camerons being presented with Colours in 1898 by Queen Victoria at Balmoral Castle when she first referred to them as 'My Own Cameron Highlanders'.

Duncan took part in this particular item as a grandchild of Queen Victoria. By this time Duncan was getting chanter lessons from John MacDougall in the band store in the evenings. But it didn't last long for, with the money he earned for his part in the Tattoo he bought a guitar. When he'd grown up, although not proficient, he could still play a good tune on the chanter and play any piece of music which was put in front of him.

This was to be my last Tattoo in Edinburgh and I enjoyed it thoroughly. Major JHL MacDonald had to ride a white horse in the Colour presentation and I used to help him put his plaid on every

151

night before the show, he would always ask about the health of the band.

During this period there were two trips to Glasgow. The first was for a television appearance on the One O'Clock Gang Show, a demented sketch and song show which the new Scottish Television channel put out every lunchtime during the week, on which personalities from different departments of the Battalion appeared. I was chosen to represent the band.

The second trip was laying up of the Colours in Glasgow Cathedral. This was a big parade, not only of the Battalion but members from the Cameron Highlanders Association, so there were many old friends to shake hands with that day.

Walt Disney was making the film Grey Friars Bobby and the band was required to take part. We were filmed at seven o'clock on a Sunday morning on the Castle Esplanade. All the pipers had to queue for makeup. When it came to my turn the makeup man when he saw my beard said

'I don't need you, but tell everybody I did it!'

The Tattoo finished on Saturday night and we were off to America for a three-month tour. We were grounded at Prestwick for twenty-four hours due to a hurricane passing through, so had to stay in a hotel overnight. However, we eventually arrived at Springfield, Massachusetts. We spent three days continually rehearsing to get everything timed to perfection. I didn't have chance to see the show from a spectators view but according to the applause we received it must have looked good, with the Military Band of the Coldstream

Guards and the Royal Stewart and Cameron tartan of the pipers and drummers of the Cameron Highlanders.

It was good fun at first but began to get tiresome having to travel all day by Greyhound bus and put on a show in the evening. The young soldiers were being fined for sleeping in and holding the buses up, some weren't even eating properly – we were responsible for our own meals. Tam Mollins was admitted to hospital for three days with ulcers. When being interviewed by a reporter with a tape recorder Tam was asked what he thought of this country, America? Tam was so ill and tired he just replied

'Ye want tae gie it back tae the Indians!'

We travelled across America, up the west coast to Canada and then back to America.

During this time an order had been issued that no alcohol would be consumed during the intermission of any show.

The night we played in Detroit was my downfall. Two ex-Camerons and Burma veterans, Jimmy Hood and John Irvine came into the dressing room after we had done an hour and thirty minutes show. They had a bottle of whisky and offered me a drink. I took the bottle and was having a swig when an officer spotted me and ordered me to return to the hotel. I changed into my civilian clothes and walked over a mile back to the hotel. I had a pocketful of dollars and there were plenty of bars where I could have stopped and got really plastered. But an order was an order.

The next day I was marched into the Major in charge of the bands and accused of being drunk. I didn't argue and he said he was sending me home. I was duly escorted to the plane by the major. I arrived at Prestwick to find two Warrant Officers waiting to escort me back to Edinburgh. Rumours were plentiful in Edinburgh about what had happened – I'd struck an officer, or I'd collapsed in the arena. I heard many stories, except the one about me just having a swig out of a bottle of whisky.

On arrival at Redford Barracks, I was marched in front of the CO. He never asked me if I had an excuse, just said

'You can have a court-martial or immediate discharge with no pension. I'll give you twenty-four hours to think it over'

Home to Molly and the children. I was a wreck and so distraught, Molly was worried so she sent for the Medical Officer.

That evening the wife of a senior officer called at the house and told me that her husband had advised that I should opt for a court-martial, as I had only fourteen months to do to qualify for a full pension, so it would be stupid to take an immediate discharge and nothing to show for all those years of loyal service. If ever I needed a friend's advice in all my service, that was one night that I appreciated it.

I was not allowed into barracks or to use the Sergeants Mess as I was confined to my married quarters.

I told the CO I wanted a court-martial, so it was a long wait for the bands to come home and all the evidence to convict me. In the meantime, I had a long letter from the Drum Major putting me in the picture. Tam Pentland's letter gave me confidence that the outcome would be in my favour. The band returned and I was eventually sent for to report to the CO's office. I was marched in and it was Major DJS Murray, second in command at the time as the CO was away, who informed me that there was insufficient evidence to put me forward for court-martial. I would be tried by the Brigadier.

I was transported to Edinburgh Castle escorted by one of my great Sergeant's Mess friends CSM Johnnie Duff, who was also my next-door neighbour in married quarters. The Major who reported me, the major in charge of the bands, was up from London and present when I was marched in front of the Brigadier, commanding Lowland District. On my own admission, I had disobeyed the Major's order, but I denied the drunk charge, telling the Brigadier I had just finished an hour and a half programme before the intermission. Maybe being a Scots Guardsman and knowing what pipers could and couldn't do, I would never know, but he seemed to have a look of understanding when I explained. The outcome was a severe reprimand for disobeying an order, the first time ever in twenty-three years service and the drunk charge was dismissed.

There were thirty-eight members of that band and if they had wished they could have said that I'd been drunk but not one did, they stood by me and I was able to shake every one of them by the hand the day I was allowed back into barracks.

I don't want the reader to think that here was a man who had never slipped up in his whole career. I did make a few mistakes during my service. The first time was during the war while I was in Inverness. That time I had slept in when I should have been playing reveille. I

155

got seven days defaulters. As part of our punishment, we had to pull a heavy roller over the Officer's Mess lawn. I had one day to go until the end of this punishment when I missed the bugle call and was late for the first defaulter parade in the morning. I received another seven days.

There were a few other minor scrapes, but the punishment was accepted. As an NCO it was normally a reprimand which remained on one's record. These records prevented me from receiving the Long Service and Good Conduct Medal.

However, this was a bitterness that remained with me for a long time after I'd left Edinburgh in 1961.

Home to Dover for Christmas leave and when I returned to Edinburgh, Major Murray was still in command. This time that I reported to him was without an escort. I was told that as I had only fourteen months to serve, there was a job in Liverpool as a Permanent Staff Instructor and that Colonel Jock Maitland-Makgill-Crichton would be delighted to have me. He wished me good luck and I had the feeling that there had been a lot of string-pulling on his part to get me to Liverpool.

It was for the best as I was going to continue teaching for the next six years.

Chapter 22 – The Liverpool Scottish and Exciseman 1961 - 1973

It was a sad day on the 25th of January 1961 when I left the Camerons. Mrs Sinclair, wife of the gentleman who fell asleep when I played Mary's Praise in the same barracks at Redford in 1948, drove us to the station. Four stalwarts got permission to play us off on the train, Tam Mollins, Alex Murray, Iain Murray and George McKendrick. Lance Corporal Andrew Venters was also being posted to the Liverpool Scottish as they always had a regular P.S.I. (Permanent Staff Instructor) Piper on the staff. His wife and daughter travelled with us and so it was quite a cheerful journey.

I had no idea what sort of reception I was going to get when I arrived in Liverpool. At the station were two Land Rovers, one to take Andy Venters and family to Woolton and the other driven by Sergeant Smith (a Cameron) to take us to Crosby. Lieutenant Colonel Maitland-Makgill-Crichton was also at the station to greet us and assured Molly that there was a nice house waiting for her in Waterloo, Crosby.

It was a nice house and beautifully furnished. The next-door neighbours, Mr and Mrs McIver had asked the people responsible for military quarters for the key so that they could have a fire lit when we arrived. They were good neighbours and we still kept in touch after we left that army house.

I was instructed to make my way into the Drill Hall the next morning at ten o'clock. There to meet me was Dougie MacIntosh, the man I was to relieve, Sandy Fleming, Harry Easton (Coco), Bob Wharton, Sergeant (Bilko) Wright and RSM Patterson, whose brother had been killed on the Irrawaddy Crossing. RSM Patterson took me to the CO and left the office. The CO asked me to sit down.

'Well Evan' he said, 'you can take over the duties from Company Sergeant Major MacIntosh, which is looking after the regular soldiers pay and help Pipe Major Daly with the Pipe Band. Now, I know you've had a big shakeup, but it is all behind you, so forget it ever happened. The only thing wrong with that tour of America was they should have sent somebody like me or David Murray in charge of the Cameron band. Someone who has known you since your boyhood days.'

This was the gentleman who used to teach us boxing in Catterick in 1938. The incident was never mentioned again. He was good to the band of the Liverpool Scottish, they all thought a lot of him and he knew them all by their nicknames.

Sam Daly said to me when I arrived

'I believe you are going to help me with the band, so I'll be happy to let you take over as I'm getting too old for the job and I'll be retiring next year anyway'

This I did and enjoyed working with them. They weren't very sure of me at first, but we soon got to know each other and I soon had them working the way I knew would be a help to their improvement.

158

On my first day at the Drill Hall, a tall man walked in, came up to me and introduced himself to me as the Drum Major. He worked as manager of a paint business a short walk from Fraser Street Drill Hall. His words were

'The last time I saw you was in the Canal Zone when you came to judge our Piping Competition at Port Said. We had a great night in the Sergeants Mess'.

I recognised him then. He was the Leading Drummer from the Scots Guards, Sergeant Bill Williams. He had retired from the Scots Guards as acting Drum Major with eleven years service. It was the Scots Guards loss and the Liverpool Scottish gain.

From the first day I saw him perform at practice with his drummers, and then on parade, I knew here is a man I can work with. He had a wonderful drum corps as good as any regular battalion and every one of his drummers could blow the bugle calls. When I would put a new tune on the board he would say

'Play it for me Pipie and I'll see if I can get a nice beating for it'.

Shades of Tam Pentland. He told me that when we did a show with the Scots Guards/Camerons in 1948 he got a lot of drumming tips from Tam Pentland.

His sense of humour also appealed to me and we were great friends for the thirteen years that I lived in Liverpool.

One particular incident I remember was when he was working at some beating with the drummers. They seemed to be having a hard

159

time getting things right. However they finally got it right, so he told the pipers to ground pipes, turn round and give the drummers a round of applause.

There were drills every Sunday and at lunchtime, the band frequented their own special pub where they would sit and have some fun. They practically took over the pub and a concert would be organised, where every member could do his party piece. Willie Fletcher would do impersonations; there were guitar players and duets. Taffy Davies doing an Irish dance while Willie Fletcher played his version of an Irish Hornpipe on the tin whistle. They would each bring sandwiches and spare ribs would be passed around. The Drum Major would also do his party piece. It wasn't long before they had Andy Venters and I involved, and we had a lot of material from our Korean days and the American tour.

What I liked about those men was the way they would be back in the Drill Hall for two o'clock and not a stagger out of any of them.

The first camp I went on with the Liverpool Scottish was at Inverness, back in the barracks again. But this time wearing the Forbes tartan but still with a Cameron badge in my hat.

Towards the end of 1961 Pipe Major Daly reminded me

'I'm retiring in June next year and you in February from the regular army. Why don't you stay in Liverpool, join as a Territorial and take over the band.'

He put this suggestion to the CO Colonel Alistair Smellie who had taken over from Colonel Maitland-Makgill-Crichton. The Colonel thought it was a good idea so when it was time to finish I organised a house for the family. We found a nice place on a quiet road in Crosby, with good neighbours and just a couple of doors from Drum Major Williams.

My regular service finished on 21st February 1962 so I joined the Liverpool Scottish. I was Private Macrae but retained my Pipe Major's badge and had the use of the Sergeants Mess until my appointment was officially granted.

That year the Liverpool Scottish went to their annual camp at Millom, Cumbria for Civil Defence training. It was at this camp that Sam Daly retired and I was promoted Sergeant, appointed Pipe Major, with pay backdated to February. Sammy was delighted that I'd got the job as Pipe Major and he presented me with a copy of Glen's Piobaireachd Collection which he'd got from Robert Reid.

During my last year as a regular soldier with the Liverpool Scottish, we used to do all sorts of jobs under RSM Patterson's direction, but we all got on well together. We would go to the Tam O'Shanter pub where we would have a couple of lunchtime pints. The army recruiting staff used to have their lunchtime pint in the same pub. Two characters who I became friendly with were Sergeant Meade of the Scots Guards and Sergeant George Shannon from the Irish Guards. George was to appear in the 1966 Anglian Television documentary All The Queens Men, a film about life in the Household Brigade, which includes the Household Cavalry, the Life Guards, Royal Horse Guards, Grenadier Guards, Scots Guards, Welsh Guards and Irish Guards.

He belonged to Bootle and when he retired he bought a house in Crosby near to where I lived. He got employed on the docks as a Checker, and I used to see quite a lot of him when I worked on the docks with Customs & Excise. He joined the Territorials and was immediately promoted to Sergeant Major of the Royal Corps of Transport (RCT).

We used to meet in our local pub The Volunteer in Waterloo and one evening I asked George if he was all prepared for camp and if his boots were polished. He replied

'My boots are highly polished, but my wife won't let me take them to camp they're so good, she's got them on the mantelpiece with flowers in them.'

This was Liverpool humour at its best which I was to hear so much of during my stay in that city.

During my days as P.S.I. Andy Venters was promoted to Corporal and he wanted to learn piobairchead and to write music. He was a good pupil and we used to have afternoon sessions in the Drill Hall.

Our wives were good friends so there were weekend visits to each other's houses. Andy worked hard at his piobaireachd and his music notation and I saw some good qualities in him for the future. He also learned a lot about soldiering as all the men he worked with were senior NCOs.

There wasn't much I could do about his future but I did have the opportunity of talking to Major Hamish Logan (Training Major with the Liverpool Scottish) about his qualifications and suggested that he

162

should have the chance of going to the Army School of Piping. Major Logan said he would see what could be done about it. Andy eventually got to the Castle and John MacLellan who was WO1 in charge of the school at that time was very pleased with him. He later became Pipe Major of the Queens Own Highlanders (amalgamated Camerons and Seaforths) and made a success of his job.

When I finished my time as a regular soldier the only work going was in security, but until something came along I was employed in the Quarter Masters Office with Captain Jack Morse and Captain Jimmie Cameron, who had been O.R.Q.M.S. (Orderly Room Quartermaster Sergeant) with us in Korea.

Eventually, I started with Securicor, but only for a while. I tried all sorts of security work but I wasn't impressed, and the hours were too long for the money offered.

At Millom Camp, we were stationed next to the Honourable Artillery Company and there were exchange visits between Sergeants Messes. Their Drum Major mentioned having been on an Edinburgh Tattoo with me. I asked him what band he'd been in. He said The Blues and Royals. I found out later that he'd been a Major in charge of the Blues.

Also in 1962, the Battalion went to Sennybridge in Wales. The band played Retreat at Llandovery and Brecon. In Brecon, we were entertained in the Club of the South Wales Borderers. One old soldier wanted to meet the two Welshmen in charge of the Scottish Band. We had been billed in the town as the Band of the Liverpool

Scottish under the direction of Drum Major William Williams and Pipe Major Evan Macrae!

The next day the band had a rest day and so went away to Swansea for an outing. I remained in camp and intended having a quiet afternoon. I was relaxing on my bed, when, about three o'clock in the afternoon the RSM's Batman knocked at my door and told me I was wanted in the Sergeants mess immediately.

The RSM at that time was Arthur Smith who had been in the Mortar Platoon in Burma and throughout his service until promotion came his way.

He met me at the door of the Sergeants Mess and said

'Get in there and look after these gentlemen! You can handle them better than I can'

Sitting at the bar were two Medical Officers, both of Irish descent. I joined their company and had some laughs and quite a few drams. The RSM knew what he was doing as he never took more than a glass of beer. Needless to say, when the Drum Major arrived back in the evening, expecting me to go to the Mess for an evening session, I'd had enough for that day.

Our next camp was at Thetford in 1964. From there the Brigade bands massed and we rehearsed for a retreat on Horse Guards Parade. The bands included The Kings Own Regiment, The South Lancashire Regiment and our Pipes and Drums of the Liverpool Scottish. The show went off well and there were congratulations from all circles. While in London we were billeted in Wellington

Barracks and Sunday lunchtime called for a visit to the Rose & Crown where we met up with some old friends.

The Brigadier at this time was Brigadier David Wilson of the Argyll and Sutherland Highlanders who took a keen interest in the Pipes and Drums.

During these camps, I was ably supported by Sergeant Massey, Corporal Glyn Pritchard and Sergeant Billy Woodward on drums. Billy had been in the Camerons as a drummer; Glyn had also been in the Camerons in Austria but not in the pipe band. He had been in the quartermasters' stores and a member of the shooting team.

Sergeant Joe Massey had some service in the Scots Guards and was very keen to learn piobaireachd so I was happy to work with him.

I never thought that I would ever play on the Esplanade at Edinburgh Castle again, but the camp at Milton Bridge, Penicuik in 1965 enabled me to do that. The band was requested to play retreat during our stay there. We also visited the Eagle Pipers Society at one of their meetings. Sergeant Joe Massey was asked to play that night. He gave a good performance finishing by playing the piobaireachd MacLeod of Raasay's Salute.

During our camp at Milton Bridge, we had a visit from Major General Maitland-Makgill-Crichton, and we had a long chat with him in the Sergeants Mess. As he was leaving, he looked round the corner of the door wearing his peaked cap braided in gold and called out

'Evan, what do you think of this?', 'Sir, you look better in a balmoral' was my reply.

The camp at Barry Buddon, Carnoustie was to be my last camp. The Territorials, as we knew it were being changed and the new setup was to be the T.A.V.R. (Territorial Army Volunteer Reserve) and there wasn't a vacancy for my rank.

Serving with the Liverpool Scottish was a happy five years for me which helped me to break away gradually from soldiering and I made a lot of new good friends in the band, the Sergeants Mess and among the officers. I kept in touch with many of those for several years.

With no band now I was approached by the Clan MacLeod Pipe Band, which I believe was first formed in 1953 by Pipe Major Angus MacLeod of the Black Watch. When I went to Liverpool in 1961 the Pipe Major was Alexander (Alec) Queen, a good piper and dancer. He had been in boy service but left as I was joining. He was captured in France with the 1st Battalion Camerons and spent four years as a P.O.W.

I took over the Clan MacLeod band and enjoyed working with them, they were all very keen and every member had to pay to be in the band. We worked hard during my first winter with them and at the end of the following season, we had a lot of success and were upgraded to Grade 3.

Unfortunately, we lost a lot of drummers the following year so I became a bit frustrated and retired from the Clan MacLeod band seemingly with nothing to aim for.

There used to be the usual weekend sessions in the Volunteer pub, Waterloo. The manager Jack Bishop being an ex-armoured corps driver and wounded in Germany loved to see ex-servicemen come into his bar. I played the pipes every year at lunchtime on New Year's day all the time I lived in Liverpool and it used to attract Scots from all over Liverpool. There would be plenty of booze and Jack always gave me a half bottle about a week after the celebrations, but never on New Year's day itself.

I applied for a job with the Customs & Excise. I got the job without having to take an exam, my army 1st Class and service being good enough to get me in as a Watcher, now called Revenue Assistant. This was my kind of job, working with ex-servicemen like Bobby Johnson ex Petty Officer and Eddie McShane. There was Joe Gillead ex-Commando, Joe Brown ex-Pipe Major of the Liverpool Scottish and Norman Foster. Norman had been badly wounded in the desert campaign and was awarded the Imperial Service Medal.

Then there were the senior officers. Mr Bultitude, the Collector, who so kindly assisted and advised me when I wanted a transfer home to the Highlands. Also, Mr Flynn who I had to report to on a Dock Station in my early days with the Excise. He sounded so gruff when I reported to him and when he asked me my name I said 'Macrae'. 'There's not many Macraes in Liverpool' he said, where are you from?'

I told him, and then he asked if I'd been in the Navy, I still had the beard. When I told him I'd been in the Queens Own Cameron Highlanders he laughed and told me a story about a cask of whisky that had been removed from the Millburn Distillery in Inverness before the war and the soldiers were suspected and investigated but nothing proved. Mr Flynn had been in the Highlands and had been sent to investigate. They were relieved to discover the forty-five-gallon cask later in the burn, but empty. The cask was more important than the contents!

Mr Flynn loved the highlands and would talk for hours about his life as an Exciseman in Scotland. I used to enjoy being on a night shift with him, as he was well-read and could discuss any subject.

The first placement I had with the Excise was in the Albert Warehouse, a huge place with long underground cellars, in which one could get lost. My boss there was Mr Duncan MacLeod who also was a thorough gentleman. His mother came from Ballachulish. Duncan was very interested in my career as a piper and the men I worked with were all fond of him.

Sometimes I wondered if the Albert Warehouse was a probationary station for men like me, to see if we could resist temptation, for a dram could always be found if one was dishonest. I never was tempted, got through my probation very quickly and was soon in uniform.

There is a pipe tune, a jig called Duncan the Gauger which I composed for Mr MacLeod and it was he who selected the name. I wanted to call it Duncan MacLeod Ballachulish.

On my last station at Gladstone Dock, I was with two gentlemen who had always been kind to me, Mr Vernon and Mr Evans.

Another great friend I had in Liverpool Docks was Alasdair MacAllister, an Excise Officer from Glasgow.

Throughout this story, one will observe that drink and booze is mentioned quite a bit. In the army, one could drink as much as one liked, provided you didn't fall all over the place, were never drunk on duty and could face the first parade in the morning without being late. Drinking was controlled by particular opening and closing hours and they were adhered to. The cure for a hangover in the army was cross country runs or route marches.

As a civilian it was different and I found myself over-indulging, which got worse as the years went by. I would still go to the pub, but not for the company. Sometimes I would shun my friends and go to a pub where I wasn't known so well. I never went home without a dram for the morning. At lunchtime on the docks, I would go out for that drink, sometimes over-do it, but because of those gentlemen in the Customs and Excise there was always somebody to cover up for me.

I had two bouts in the hospital with chest pains and a warning from the doctor about liver damage. I was never physically aggressive with my family and I never left Molly short of money, but the mental strain on her must have been terrible. However, and thankfully, she stuck it out in the hope that one day I would come to my senses.

What was happening to me? My body would crave for whisky and I wouldn't eat for weeks. I remained tidy in my uniform, always a clean white shirt every day and boots highly polished.

But still that sickness!

I would go to work in the morning but wouldn't come home until the pubs closed. If Molly shouted at me it made me all the more determined to keep drinking. I knew I was doing wrong but how was I to get away from it all. I thought of the church but that would be no good. I thought of Alcoholics Anonymous, but I thought – I wasn't an alcoholic!

I rose early one Saturday morning feeling terrible and having bought a bottle of whisky the night before started drinking from it, but it wasn't making me feel better.

Molly came downstairs, she didn't shout, she just said

'Oh Evan, not at this time of the morning, you must be ill'

I was shattered and broke down. Molly asked

'Will I go and see Wally?'

Wally was someone I used to drink with but who had gone sober.

Wally arrived and spoke in his quiet voice

'Do you want to get sober Evan' he asked.

I nodded so he said

'The first thing we do is pour this down the sink', so away went my bottle.

Wally sat with me all day and all evening.

He kept in touch with me until he could take me to a meeting of Alcoholics Anonymous.

I will be forever grateful to Wally who showed me the way to sobriety and eventually a life of peace. I also owe a lot to Bill and Harry who used to come to my house every Monday evening for two hours piobaireachd lessons and an hour or two about the benefits of being sober. They helped someone who couldn't handle booze any more.

I know in AA one is supposed to preserve their anonymity, so I've only used the first names of those who first helped me, but I am not ashamed to admit that I had got help.

I had been drinking from the age of eighteen and I don't blame anyone for my drinking. I believe in the saying, you can lead a horse to water but you can't make him drink. Maybe some young piper might read this book and think – take care.

When I decided to stop drinking I said to Molly that I'm not going to be a hermit. In nine months I had a new car and was taking trips to Edinburgh to listen to piping competitions. I also had a lift up to the Cowal Games in Dunoon. We'd left early on the Saturday morning after I'd been on the docks all night on duty. I slept all the way up to Glasgow.

New Year would be the trial period. Would I survive?

Duncan MacLeod had retired from the Excise and asked if I would play in his Golf Club in Prenton at Hogmanay. He also knew I'd gone sober and that he would look after me. I had to play the new Captain of the Golf Club and the retiring Captain into the hall when a tray of drinks came out. Duncan whispered to me,

'take the one next to the waiter's thumb'

It was dry ginger, trust an Exciseman.

The next day, 1st January was the day I would normally be playing in the Volunteer pub. Jack Bishop knew I had gone sober and was delighted when I did appear. I survived the three hours in the pub playing my pipes without a drink. Molly was very apprehensive about me going, but when I returned home not having taken a drink she knew I was on the way to a new life.

Summer came and it was a holiday home to Nairn. I was back in the Highlands again but seeing them differently. I asked Molly's parents that if we should decide to come home to Scotland, could they put us up until such times as we got a place of our own. They were only too pleased to help.

Back in Liverpool and work, I put my application in for a transfer to any distillery near Nairn and I had to name them in order of preference. Two weeks after my application was submitted a vacancy was advertised for Invergordon. Mr Bultitude advised me to take it, as he said; you may wait years for another one, those highlanders hang on for a long time.

Chapter 23 – Customs & Excise Inverness 1973 - 1974

By November 5th we were on our way. We had an overnight stay in Edinburgh with ex Drum Major MacDonald and his wife Jenny. The snow was on the hills as we drove up the A9 and we arrived in Nairn on Molly's birthday. She said it was the best birthday present she ever had. She was back home in Nairn with a sober husband on 6th November 1973.

I had to report to Invergordon Distillery at 9 a.m. on Monday morning and was introduced to the fellows I was to work with. One of them was a relative of the wife of John D Burgess. He gave me their address in Ardross so I called to see them one evening. John was pleased to see me and the following night as I was on my way home to Nairn, they very kindly offered me a room to stay in during the week and just return to Nairn at the weekend. This was a handy arrangement and I used to enjoy the long evening talks with John and Sheila. Some evenings we would have a tune on our pipes, but it was difficult trying to start all over again. John suggested I should keep my kilt and jacket at his place in case something might crop up and I might be asked to play.

I arrived home at John's house at half-past five one evening and he said to me

'How would you like a job like mine?'

John was teaching in the schools in Easter Ross. I said I'd love it so he said he'd phone Inverness for an application form which arrived the next day.

The vacancy was in Lochaber. What better place for a Cameron to teach bagpipes, the home of the Regiment, Fort William.

There were two piping jobs for me to do while I lived with John. One evening he said to me before my evening meal

'Don't eat too much, you are playing at a Burns Supper tonight'

I said that I thought he was going to do that job, but he explained that the car accident he'd had a few days earlier was playing him up and he'd been to the doctor, who advised more rest.

'Don't worry' he said, 'Sheila's pressed your kilt and jacket, I've polished your shoes and pipes, the pipes are going well, and you'll be picked up at seven o'clock'

Arriving home to Nairn one evening I phoned Colonel Douglas Miers and told him that I'd applied for a job in Lochaber and that I'd used his name as a reference. He said he'd be delighted to do so.

I'd remembered meeting him at the Northern Meetings after I'd changed my lifestyle and speaking to him. He'd asked me what I was doing and I told him that I was with the Customs and Excise in Liverpool. His reply that day was

'You should get yourself a job like Burgess'

Not long after I'd moved home to Nairn and was working at Invergordon I had a message from the young Colonel Miers asking me to play at his father's funeral. The church in Inverness was packed the day of the funeral and there were lots of well known Cameron Officers there. The interment at Tomnahurich Cemetery was family only, where I played Lochaber No More. Mrs Miers approached me after the graveside service and said,

'If Colonel Ronnie had known that you would play the pipes at his   funeral, he would have been pleased'

I also submitted Captain John MacLellan's name for a reference as he had known me longer than anybody who was still in piping circles.

One other person who gave me a reference and sent a copy to me was the Reverend Gordon Glen. He was from Ayrshire and his wife was from Argyll. Mrs Glen had heard about me when I was in Liverpool and came to my house there and asked if I would teach their son Ian. I'd said I would and taught him for six years. He became very proficient and I wanted to take him to the Clan MacLeod Band. I had three other boys who used to compete at the S.P.B.A. competitions and at the annual Blackpool Games. They were two brothers Shacklady and Robin Scott, the latter's father having served in Korea as a cook.

Ian explained that he couldn't get involved as he was attending Merchant Taylor's School and had a lot of studies to do, so he would practice his chanter at home or have a blow at his pipes. He said this would relax him and he could approach his studies with a different mind. This was a tip I would use when I taught the youngsters at Fort

175

William. Whenever I asked them if they have been practicing, some would answer

'No, I've been studying for my O Levels'

I would then advise them to keep the chanter handy and take some time to play a tune while doing their homework. This was a tip an old hand had learned from a young one.

An interview was arranged in Inverness and I was accepted for the job as Piping Instructor in part of the Lochaber area. I duly handed in my notice at the Excise and started my new job on 1st April 1974.

Chapter 24 – Piping in Lochaber 1974 - 1987

I had no idea what I was letting myself in for. All I knew was I wanted to teach pipes. I was given seven Primary Schools to visit and the Lochaber High School. What would the headmasters think, would they accept me, and would they put any snags in my way? I needn't have worried. I got all the help I wanted from every one of them and continued to do so during my time teaching.

Alec MacDonald, the Station Master at Fort William, had a small band going when I arrived which was called the Lochaber Junior Pipe Band. This was all done in his spare time, but he made a good little band out of them. Alec had served in the Highland Brigade I.T.C (Infantry Training Centre) with Donald MacLean of the Seaforths. He had also spent some time with the Gordon Highlanders and had served under Pipe Major George Wilson, my old friend from the Victory Parade days. But I didn't get to know Alec until he had joined the 4/5th Camerons. I met them both when they came to Liverpool to do a massed bands retreat with the Liverpool Scottish. Alec welcomed me to Fort William and told me how pleased he was that I'd got the job and that I was just the man to help him with his band.

We worked out a system, that when a youngster had reached a required standard they would join the band, with their parents' permission. At that time we had a little room in Fort William to

177

practice in but when I saw how big we were going to be, I realised that something had to be done.

The headmaster in the High School, Mr MacWilliam, was approached and gave his permission for us to use the High School two nights a week. We eventually changed our name to the Lochaber High School Pipe Band, with Alec still Pipe Major. I would supply the pipers and act as Secretary/Treasurer. The drummers were well taught by Donald McLeod who had also been in the 4/5th Camerons. Not even in my army days had I seen anybody teach drummers so quickly and in no time have them on parade.

When I look back I can't help thinking about how good life had become, it was a wonderful time working with these youngsters, learning band tunes, learning piobaireachd and preparing them for competitions. They had so much trust in me. They would include me in their Christmas card list and those that knew my birthday never forgot to send me a card.

The names of all those youngsters are too numerous to mention, but to every one of them I say, thank you for making an old soldier so happy.

I lodged with my niece Morag until I could get a house and I used to go to Alec's house for a blow. One day he asked me if I was going to compete. I said I don't think so as I hadn't competed in the North since 1947. However, Alec was a cousin of Bob Nicol of Ballater who had been piper/gamekeeper to the Royal Family for over forty years but was now retired. Arrangements were made for me to meet Bob. I didn't know how I was going to get on with Bob; I knew he had gone to John MacDonald for twenty years. On my first visit, he asked me to play something then remarked

'There's nothing wrong with your playing, just a bit rusty'

I would go to Ballater every Saturday as long as I could get over Tomintoul.

In 1975 I went to see Bob and played my four piobaireachds for the upcoming Northern Meetings.

Bob said

'If you play any of your tunes like that at Inverness I'm sure you'll be on the prize list'

I got the tune Fair Honey to play and was on the prize list.

I began to enjoy my competitions then, as I was getting over the nerves which many pipers suffer from and I kept receiving plenty of tunes on tape from Bob. On each Saturday he would be waiting for me outside a little cafe in Ballater where we would have lunch, then back to his house for a four-hour session on piobaireachd.

I think he enjoyed my visits as much as I did, as he would phone Alec and ask

'Is young Macrae coming over on Saturday?'

I was over 50 then!

The last time I visited Bob was in 1978; he was very ill and getting over a serious operation but he still insisted I come over. He met me in his pyjamas and dressing gown and we talked about the medal tunes and went over them on the chanter.

His brother David and wife were looking after him and as he was so ill and tired he had to go to bed. I was about to leave when David told me not to go as Bob wanted to hear me play my tunes for the Gold Medal Competition, while he slept. He woke up and asked me to come into his bedroom and play my four tunes on the pipes. One of them was MacDougal's Gathering, and ill as he was he reached out for his chanter and demonstrated the double echo movement. Two days later Bob had passed away.

Two stalkers from Balmoral with Captain Andrew Pitkeathly of the Argylls and I carried his coffin the last part of the journey to the graveside where this great man now rests, as Jimmy MacGregor played. There were many of Bob Nicol's pupils attending the funeral that day. I had seen Bob quite a lot and heard him play, but I only got to know him well in the four years that I would visit him on those special Saturdays. He was a good man and a great loss to the piping community.

The encouragement Bob gave me enabled me to attend as many competitions as I could get to and I began to enjoy them. It was wonderful visiting many highland games, meeting old friends, going back to the Portree Games and staying in Harlosh, Skye with the Laing family for three days with a pipers' gathering every night. This was something I never imagined in my Liverpool days, would ever happen again.

I was asked to call into the Council Offices in Fort William. I met a man Ballatyne in charge of the housing department and allocation. He asked if I was the Macrae who was a friend of Willie Manson. When I said I was he laughed

'That was a good five days we had in Brora 1947'

He gave me the address of the house I was to live in so I went to view it. Going around the back of the house who should I see looking at me but Bill Davie who was O.R.Q.M.S with the 79th P.T.C and with the 1st Battalion in Tripoli, until he took ill and was sent home.

Bill and his wife became good neighbours and he and I talked a lot about the Camerons. He joined the Regiment in 1931 serving in India, Khartoum and Palestine before the 2nd World War started.

I was befriended by many pipers in Fort William and the surrounding areas. One man I remember fondly was Sandy Masson, the Gamekeeper at Mamore near Kinlochleven. Sandy called at the house to have his bagpipes seen to. Molly was home baking and said that I shouldn't have any as I was getting too fat. Sandy said

'A day out on the hills would do you good'

I said I'd love it so it was arranged that I go out with him during the hind season, which continued for three years. Great days out on the hill hearing Sandy talk about the animals and their habits, then home in the evening to a big meal from Jane his wife and of course a blow on the pipes. He was a great man dedicated to his job and a great sense of humour. He eventually became Head Stalker on the Royal

Estate at Balmoral. (Note added: Sandy was awarded MVA (Member of the Royal Victorian Order) in the 1997 New Year's Honours.)

In 1976 my first granddaughter Catherine was born. I didn't get a chance to see her when she was born as Duncan and family were living in Menorca and at the end of that summer season, they moved to Mallorca. A few months later Duncan along with some friends decided they would hold a charity fancy dress 'tramps' ball. Coincidentally it was to be the same week as 25th January that year so they thought it would a good idea to combine it with a Burns night celebration. I was asked to fly over for the night, Saturday, and bring a haggis with me. It was also an opportunity for me to meet my first granddaughter. The plan was for me to play the haggis in and offer the usual Toast to the Haggis. I mentioned to Alec MacDonald that I wouldn't be at band practice Friday or see the band play in the town as I was going to play pipes at a Burns Supper in Spain. Alec thought I'd said I was playing at a Burns Supper in Spean! Of course, he reminded me there were no public parties in Spean Bridge that Saturday. I had to repeat that I was going to Spain for the night, not Spean!

Anyway, Duncan organised a flight for me from Glasgow and when I arrived at Palma Airport, Pipes in the box, with a huge haggis stuffed inside the Spanish Police were more concerned about the haggis than the pipes. I had not long stopped drinking and was worried about how I'd cope with the temptation. But Duncan was very helpful and made sure I was only offered dry ginger.

The next morning Sunday another flight was organised for me with Thomsons to fly back to Glasgow. It was a great 2 days and I enjoyed meeting my granddaughter for the first time.

When I was in the hospital for my operation Molly came to visit and we were chatting away when she noticed a man in a bed down the row. He was bandaged and splinted quite heavily. Molly asked me what had happened to him. I replied that he fell of the Ben, meaning Ben Nevis. Molly thought I'd said 'bed' and remarked

"'Oh yes the beds are quite high aren't they?"

After we'd settled in Fort William I felt I needed a side hobby, so bringing to mind the skills and patience of John MacDonald the Ardvasar Blacksmith that I'd so admired I decided I fancied making pipe chanter and drone reeds. I fitted out the shed in the back garden with as many tools as I would need for the task and spent many happy peaceful hours whittling and turning and polishing. I even had a go at making a few fiddles.

We had an internal intercom system set up from the kitchen to the shed so that Molly could contact me without having to come out in the rain.

One evening while I was in the shed, a chap knocked at the door and asked Molly if Jock was in. She replied

" yes, come in, I'll get him for you"

I was known by quite a few people, particularly from Liverpool as Jock. He sat down and Molly made him a cup of tea. She then called me on the intercom that there was someone here to see me. There were always people calling – old comrades, pupils, friends, either for a tune on the pipes, a chat about old times, or to pick up some reeds. There was nothing unusual about my current visitor.

Anyway, when I came into the room, we all looked at each other in silence and Molly pointed at our visitor,

"This man is here to see you, Evan"

The man stood up and quickly said

"you're not Jock!".

He'd knocked at the wrong door!

As I write, I occasionally look through my scrapbook and I come across many invitations to Officers weddings over the years, for I was always delighted to be asked to play. For me, as well as the Bridegroom, this was a big day. I'll name here some of the officers but not in order of seniority, but just as they appear in the scrapbook.

Major A. Findlay (later Brigadier) Captain D.A.N.C Miers (later Colonel), Major John Villiers Stuart, Mr D.G.MacDonald, Mr John Jersey MacLeod and Captain A.A. Fairrie (later Lieutenant Colonel).

Major Findlay was married at the Royal Military Chapel in Sandhurst. I was given accommodation in the Sergeants Quarters. RSM Lord would not let me have a drink at the bar until I gave him a tune on the pipes. On the Sunday, he requested or practically ordered me to be a spectator at a parade of the Cadets. After the parade he had me stand at the door of the Mess and the Sergeants' wives had to kiss the man with the beard before they were allowed into the Mess.

At Captain Miers' wedding, people in London must have thought these highlanders were mad. The guests were dancing a sixteen-some reel on the lawn by the side of the Thames. That day I changed in the beer cellar of the Rose & Crown. I asked the boss had he seen any of my Scots Guards friends, he replied 'Not lately'

He'd hardly finished responding when Curly Roe and Bob Kilgour walked through the door. They were playing at a Guards Officer's wedding in Chelsea and were doing the same as me, using the pub to change into uniform and tune their pipes.

Meanwhile, two Cameron Officers passing a church in Chelsea saw pipers through the door and thought they'd arrived. When they entered the church and about to sit down, they realised they were in the wrong church.

I was in the Liverpool Scottish when I played at Mr Jersey MacLeod's wedding and it was good to see all my old Cameron friends again. Dougie MacLeod was the family piper and we both played at the wedding.

A Spanish waiter at the Reception came on to the veranda and offered me champagne, but Dougie explained that wasn't the drink for pipers. The waiter returned with a bottle of whisky. Some of the officers came out and asked

'What have the pipers got that we haven't'

185

'Whisky' replied Dougie

One evening in 1966 in Liverpool while sitting at home, nothing to do, the doorbell rang. When I answered it, there stood Captain Fairrie and his fiancée inviting me to play at their wedding at Much Hadham, Hertfordshire in April. On arrival for the wedding, I was met at the station, taken to the gardener's cottage and given a room to change. In the room was a tray with a half bottle of whisky and a glass. At the time I thought very thoughtful of some old soldier. While I was tuning my pipes in the room I saw Lieutenant General P. M. Hunt having a stroll I suppose. At this time he was Colonel of the Queens Own Highlanders (Seaforth and Camerons). He was in a morning suit with his head down deep in thought. I played the Cameron Men in step with his stride. He stopped to wonder where the sound was coming from, and then just continued.

The last wedding I played at in connection with the Cameron Highlanders was for Colonel David Murray's daughter Alison. The Colonel wrote to me from Singapore and invited me to play. The wedding was to be in Lingfield. I used the same room as Colonel Murray to change into uniform. The Colonel was dressed and he saw me looking at him.

'Don't look like that Pipie. We've all got to do what we're told'

He wasn't wearing a Cameron kilt.

These were functions at which I enjoyed meeting Officers I'd met over the years. They never failed to stop and shake hands and maybe dig up some story from the past.

186

It was difficult trying to keep sober when old pals would come to my house. The parents of the Lochaber juniors never said anything but they were pleased when they knew I'd changed my lifestyle on returning to Scotland. I was doing something I liked doing and being paid for it.

It had taken six months of illness, hospitalisation and operation to make me sit down and think of writing this story. I've named officers, sergeants, pipers and people I've worked with, but there are many others, too numerous to mention. I've met them through piping all over the world and we still kept in touch up to the end.

My operation was successful and by the time I'd finished writing these memoirs I was back at work looking forward to the Juniors competing, preparing myself for competition and hearing the band practice for the summer season.

They would normally play two nights a week and entertain the locals and visitors in Fort William.

Sheesh Gilles, from my days in Burma, will be there, he never misses a performance, and he'll remember some event from India or Burma. Sheesh was more afraid of the RSM than he was of the Japanese.

He'll ask me

'Is the band playing Over The Chindwin tonight, Pipie?'

Postscript

By

Duncan Macrae

Evan finished writing his memoirs towards the end of 1981, and although his book is about his piping life and career he fails to include his achievements in the piping arena. I felt it was appropriate to resolve his humble oversight and cover that here.

When he moved to Fort William in 1974 to become the area school's piping tutor he then started competing more regularly. He had already entered for the Northern Meeting competition in 1973, before moving from Liverpool but he was not placed.

However, in the next 10 years, he competed in several competitions, The Northern Meeting, Argyllshire Gathering, Skye Highland Games, Strathpeffer Highland Games, British Legion Competition, Edinburgh Police Piping Competition and the Eagle Pipers Competition.

The information below was provided by Jeannie Campbell of the Piping Times. We have a photo of Evan competing at the Nairn Games in 1979, which is not listed here. It is possible he competed in other competitions which have not been recorded.

1973	Northern Meeting	Entered, not placed, address in Liverpool
1975	Argyllshire Gathering	2nd in March
	Northern Meeting	4th Gold Medal, playing Fair Honey
	British Legion Competition	1st Confined March(restricted to those who had not won before or any other major piping competition in Scotland)
	Skye Games	2nd Captain Kemble Challenge Star
1976	Northern Meeting	Entered, not placed, address in Fort William
1977	Northern Meeting	Entered, not placed
	Skye Games	4th Dunvegan Medal
1978	Argyllshire Gathering	Entered Gold Medal playing MacDougals Gathering, not placed
1979	Argyllshire Gathering	Entered Gold Medal competition, not placed
	Northern Meeting	4th Gold Medal playing The Groat
	Strathpeffer Highland Games	Winner Invercharron Brooch
1980	Argyllshire Gathering	Gold Medal playing Isobel MacKay, not placed
	Northern Meeting	Entered, not placed
	British Legion Competition	3rd Piobaireachd, 4th March, 4th Strathspey&Reel
	Edinburgh Police Competition	3rd Piobaireachd
	Eagle Pipers Competition	Entered, not placed
1981	Argyllshire Gathering	Gold Medal playing Kings Taxes, not placed

	Northern Meeting	5th Gold Medal playing Squinting Patrick
	British Legion Competition	3rd Piobaireachd, won QOH Silver Jug for piobaireachd, 3rd Strathspey&Reel
1982	Argyllshire Gathering	1st Gold Medal playing Sqinting Patrick
	Northern Meeting	4th Gold Medal, playing Macrae's March
1983	Northern Meeting	Entered Gold Medal & The Clasp, not placed

He competed at least 20 times coming first in 3 competitions, the major one being the Oban Gold in 1982 and he was placed in several others.

After the operation on his back, he went back to work, teaching the youngsters of Lochaber and continue to compete until 1984 when he was asked to judge the piping at various competitions. He did this until 1990. In his retirement, he also found a passion for making chanter and pipe reeds, which he was shipping to pipers all over the world. He even turned his hand to making fiddles.

He also composed many pipe tunes which he has not mentioned,

Over The Chindwin (6/8 March),

This tune was composed in December 1944 by PM Evan Macrae, 1st Bn The Queen's Own Cameron Highlanders, to commemorate the crossing of the River Chindwin in Upper Burma by the 1st Camerons at the beginning of the final campaign in Burma.

Prince Charles' Welcome to Lochaber (2/4 March),

Composed by PM Evan Macrae to commemorate the visit to Lochaber by HRH Prince Charles, Prince of Wales, Duke of Rothesay and Lord of the Isles.

The Duirnish Piping Society (Strathspey),

The Piping Society at Duirinish, Skye, was formed by Dr. Tony Fisher in 1971 to help and encourage young pipers in the district. He was assisted by Angus MacLeod from Dundee. At many of the recitals Colonel Jock Macdonald, Viewfield, was Chairman for the evening. PM Evan Macrae composed this tune for the Society of which he was made an Honorary Member.

Michael Joseph MacKinnon (2/4 March),

Composed by PM Evan Macrae for Michael Joseph MacKinnon, a personal friend in Barra, who is well known as a clarsach maker. He was in the Merchant Navy, and in World War II was captured in the Indian Ocean and held as a prisoner of war in Germany. His two grand-daughters are pipers and have been pupils of PM Macrae

The Ardvasar Blacksmith (Reel),

This tune was composed by Evan as a tribute to John MacDonald who taught him the pipes as a boy, before he left Skye in 1938 to join The Queen's Own Cameron Highlanders. John MacDonald is a nephew of the famous Calum Mor (Malcolm MacInnes, who published collections of bagpipe and traditional Highland music) and he was taught the pipes by Ross, the late Lord MacDonald of MacDonald's family piper at Armadale Castle.

John MacDonald was well known as a Skye personality whose life style had never changed. He ran the croft in the way he was taught as a boy. He walked two miles to Church at Kilmore each Sunday, where he was the precentor (a person whose duty it is to lead the congregation in the singing of psalms). He kept his forge in working order for many years, although there were no horses left to be shod

Colonel Robertson MacLeod's Farewell to Tulliallan (4/4 March).

Col. R.C. Robertson-MacLeod, DSO, MC, TD served in The Queen's Own

Cameron Highlanders from 1939 until transferring to The King's Own Scottish Borderers in 1950. He won the MC with the 4th Camerons in France in 1940 before being taken prisoner with 51st Highland Division at St. Valery, and won the DSO for gallantry while serving with the 1st King's Own Scottish Borderers in Korea. After leaving the Army he became Commandant of the Scottish Police College Tulliallan from 1966 to 1979. This tune was composed in 1979 by PM Evan Macrae, late Cameron Highlanders, to mark Col. Robertson-Macleod's retirement.

The Liverpool Scottish Salute to 'Tiny' Barber (Slow March)

This tune was composed by PM Evan MacRae as a tribute to Lieutenant General Sir Colin Barber, KBE, CB, DSO, DL who was Honorary Colonel of The Liverpool Scottish from 1948-1964. General Barber was originally commissioned in the Liverpool Scottish in 1916 and subsequently in The Queen's Own Cameron Highlanders. His final appointment was as GOC in C Scottish Command and Governor of Edinburgh Castle. He was affectionately known as 'Tiny' because of his height of 6 foot 9 inches, and was the tallest officer in the Army. He died in 1964.

Alec MacDonald – Fort William (Reel)

Alec MacDonald was once a Gordon Highlander and completed his working career as the stationmaster at Fort William. The composer wanted to dedicate a tune to Alec who selected this one from a selection Evan had written but not named. Both men were involved in teaching the Lochaber High School Pipe Band.

Mrs. Cath MacDonald (Hornpipe)

Composed for the wife of a Gordon Highlander who lived in Fort William. Mrs. Cath MacDonald is the wife of Alexander MacDonald the stationmaster at Fort William.

Blackwater Dam Graves (Slow Air)

The Blackwater Reservoir is ten miles east of Kinlochleven and was completed in 1907. Once when out stalking there about 1976 with Sandy Masson, who was then the Head Keeper at Balmoral, the composer came upon the graves and his friend told him that they were mainly of Irish people who had died whilst building the dam for the Reservoir. There were nineteen graves in all including a woman's and the composer writes, 'I had this lament in my mind from that day onwards.'

Duncan The Gauger (Jig)

Evan composed this jig for Mr Duncan MacLeod from Ballachulish.
He worked with Duncan in the Customs & Excise. A gauger is a
customs officer who inspects bulk merchandise, esp liquor casks, for
excise duty purposes. Duncan chose the name though Evan wanted to
call it Duncan MacLeod Ballachulish.

Iain MacFadyen Junior (Jig)

Iain is the son of Iain MacFadyen the well known piper and tutor.
Young Iain attended an Easter class at the Sabhal Mor in Skye where
Evan taught each year. The Pipe Major writes, 'I was amused at the
way he marched and played as it reminded me of his father who
served with me in the Camerons.'

John MacKenzie's Farewell To Lochaber High School (Slow Air)

John MacKenzie was Deputy Headmaster of Lochaber High School
and a friend of Evan. The day before John MacKenzie was due to
retire Evan MacRae was asked to compose a tune for him and he
writes, 'It was a rushed job. I didn't think much of it at the time but
Alec MacDonald, the stationmaster at Fort William, encouraged me
to teach it to the school band and the more I heard it the more I liked
it!'

Alex MacLeod's farewell to Caol School

Alex taught at Caol Primary School from 1963 to 1988 when he retired as headmaster. He was instrumental in introducing the chanter to the children and Evan took those classes. Evan wrote this tune to commemorate Alex's retirement from teaching in 1988

Loch Treig (Reel)

Named after a lovely loch which lies east of Fort William and north east of Luibeilt.

Mamore (Strathspey)

Mamore, an attractive though rugged estate situated to the south east of Fort William, is now owned by the British Aluminium Company. Sandy Masson, who became Head Keeper at Balmoral and a close friend of the composer, was Head Keeper at Mamore when they first met. He invited Evan MacRae to stalk on the estate and as the composer says, 'these were enjoyable days for me as I had missed the exercise after leaving the Army'.

Sandy Masson (March)

At the time of composition Sandy Masson was the Head Keeper at Balmoral and Evan wrote, 'I first met Sandy Masson when I had a winter class for adults in 1975. He was interested in advancing his piping standard. Whilst talking he asked me if I was interested in stalking and that he could arrange for a day on the hills during the hind season. This built up a great friendship and every winter until such times as he went to Balmoral, I would go out with him. He was always interesting and would talk for hours on wild life and nature and of course had a great sense of humour. A great man and worthy of a tune.'

Rector James MacWilliam, Lochaber High School (Retreat March)

Dedicated to a Rector who takes a great interest in the School Pipe Band and the progress of each individual junior competing piper.

Lieutenant Colonel Grant-Peterkin's Farewell (played as March or Slow Air)

This was composed by Evan Macrae to commemorate Lt. Col. Grant Peterkin's leaving the Battalion from their posting in Austria/Germany

Pipe Major Bob Slater (3/4 Retreat March)

Evan met Pipe Major Bob Slater of the 8th Gordon Highlanders while serving in Burma. They were good friends and Bob taught Evan the Football Song which Evan used as his party piece for years later.

The Sabhal Mor Primrose (Slow Air)

Written by Evan to honour the work of Christine Primrose MBE, a Gaelic singer and music teacher in Skye. She has a degree in traditional Gaelic music, and she has been performing all around the world

Craighill

Written by Evan as a gift to Lt Colonel Angus Fairrie whose home was named Craighill on the Black Isle

He's even had pipe tunes named after him –

Pipe Major Evan Macrae (composer P/M J.S.Roe),

Evan Macrae's Beard (composer P/M Jack Chisolm)

Evan MacRae's March to Ft. Sherman (composer Bruce Gandy, Canada)

Evan Macrae's Favourite (composer Iain MacPherson MM)

Pipe Major Evan Macrae , Queen's Own Highlanders (composer William J Watt)

Finally, most fittingly, in 1987 he was awarded the BEM (British Empire Medal) for services to piping.

Printed in Great Britain
by Amazon